Working with Video Gamers and Games in Therapy

Working with Video Gamers and Games in Therapy moves beyond stereotypes about video game addiction and violence to consider the role that games play in psychological experiences and mental health. Chapters examine the factors that compel individual gamers to select and identify with particular games and characters, as well as the different play styles, genres, and archetypes common in video games. For clinicians looking to understand their clients' relationships with video games or to use games as a therapeutic resource in their own practice, this is a thoughtful, comprehensive, and timely resource.

Anthony M. Bean, PhD, is a licensed psychologist and executive director at The Telos Project, a non-profit mental health clinic in Fort Worth, Texas, and an adjunct professor at Framingham State University in Massachusetts. He specializes in the therapeutic implications of video games and gaming, working with children and adolescents, and the use of video-game character identification as a therapeutic technique.

Working with Video Gamers and Games in Therapy

A Clinician's Guide

ANTHONY M. BEAN

Routledge
Taylor & Francis Group

NEW YORK AND LONDON

First published 2018
by Routledge
711 Third Avenue, New York, NY 10017

and by Routledge
2 Park Square, Milton Park, Abingdon, Oxon, OX14 4RN

Routledge is an imprint of the Taylor & Francis Group, an informa business

Library of Congress Cataloging-in-Publication Data
A catalog record for this title has been requested

ISBN: 978-1-138-74712-8 (hbk)
ISBN: 978-1-138-74714-2 (pbk)
ISBN: 978-1-315-17338-2 (ebk)

Typeset in Avenir and Dante
by Florence Production, Ltd, Stoodleigh, Devon, UK

To my loving wife, Holiday, and
amazing son August.

Also,

For all of those who believe playing video games
is a waste of time—read and weep.

Contents

Introduction

1

Video games have emerged as the number one pastime activity for the past decade, or even longer for some, overtaking extracurricular, reading, and other less pleasurable activities by storm for all ages. Everyone has heard about video games and usually is, on a basic level, familiar with the different types of video games available. With the younger generations playing for fun, the middle-aged playing for a break or passing time at home or work, and the elderly playing to keep their minds sharp to stave off dementia; video games have become a distinct part of every culture and age range. The evolving state of virtual worlds and video games creates a future where the imagination is the only limitation. The virtual worlds themselves can be exciting or have disastrous consequences, both for the real life of the video gamer or the avatar being controlled. This book discusses video gamers, and the worlds they play in, through an experiential and academic viewpoint. Most of the time, researchers, politicians, families, therapists, and society view video gaming as detrimental to the human population (Anderson & Bushman, 2001; Dill & Dill, 1998). These accusations are usually created upon unfounded and biased statements with little factual data bolstering the claims (Ferguson, 2007). However, the allegations continue to exist and video gamers are portrayed in a negative light due to these stereotypes. This negative framework is not necessarily or inherently bad, but is only a small percentage, at best, of understanding why people are attracted to these experiences and most definitely not fully attributable to the video gamer population. This information makes it seem as if society and culture completely misunderstands what constitutes and comprises a video gamer, suggesting a review of our own biases, preconceived notions, and attitudes to an activity which most of us participate in every day (Granic et al., 2014).

This book focuses on understanding video games, video gamers, the virtual worlds, and current research which may not be as prevalent as the current video game violence debate found in social media, the nightly news, and news articles (Bean et al., 2017; Ferguson, 2013). Furthermore, it proceeds to understand the video gamer from a different viewpoint, enriching the narrative of the video gamer itself. The primary theoretical framework employed within this book is of a Humanistic and Jungian/Archetypal paradigm of thought, but is academic in nature. For individuals not familiar with these paradigms, it is not necessary to have more than a basic conceptualization of the theories. This lens and framework coupled with experience as a psychologist creates a new and improved way of viewing video gamers, their habits, and how to understand them in multiple settings, differing from an addiction perspective, which is currently held in fascination by many therapists and mental health workers.

As of the current DSM-5 it is listed as a possible disorder stemming from addictive behaviors, cognitions, and lack of social adjustments (APA, 2013). Even more recently, the World Health Organization (WHO) has prematurely labeled video gaming as an addictive disorder (WHO, 2016a; 2016b). This perspective is exceptionally limited in scope because it stems from a primary behavioral perspective based off of criteria of substance abuse which is significantly different than what video gamers are experiencing (Aarseth et al., 2016; Bean et al., 2017). This book places an importance on viewing the video gamer and the different realms as a different space in which to grow, fantasize, and explore, without the general stereotypes to follow through an academic and therapeutic lens, allowing a deeper and more holistic understanding of the video gamer to unfold.

Use of video games has been continuously growing across the world; every year more and more people play video games. Some scholars and advocates may say individuals play video games because they are "addicted to technology" or "enjoy the violence." Others retort the importance of the imaginative experiences pursued within these digital environments. Still more see little to no harm in playing video games, while others believe them to cause aggressive tendencies within individuals (Anderson & Bushman, 2001; Anderson & Dill, 2000). The experiences found within the video games themselves and imparted upon the video gamer contain numerous and various virtual worlds which are abundant and expansive in their design and play. Some video gamers prefer to participate in one capacity or play in the virtual world while other's play for other motives or incentives. Every conceived virtual world has a story to tell, a life to experience, and controls to master. With the continual induction of video games, virtual worlds, and augmented reality into our general lives, one may say it would be difficult to imagine a life without them. Thinking of the current growing generation, most children these days are brought up with technology and have a much greater versatility than their parents, or even half a generation before them. Technology continues to grow, expand, and explore new concepts and expand the fringes of imagination; this includes video games.

While the video games industry views video games as entertainment—and they are correct in this manner that video games do provide a form of entertainment—scholars, such as myself, purport the idea that video games can be important, provide emotional experiences, social activity, and interaction while stimulating the senses socially (Granic et al., 2014; Bean et al., 2017). By playing the video game and participating in the virtual world, someone is in fact playing around in another's imagination. The video game itself is the work of usually dozens of people's imaginations, working in harmonious sync with one another, that the video gamer has the opportunity to play through. Through this imaginative play, a person connects with the characters, the authors of the video game, and participates in something meaningful outside of the usual confined space of an individual's immediate world. Furthermore, this evocative experience in which one is actively participating in is also being shared across thousands of other individuals. Other people playing the same video game are additionally experiencing the same mechanisms, literacy, and development as the current player while fostering different styles of game play; and all of this is happening without interaction between people!

As such, it is easy to wonder about the influence video games have upon an individual's psyche or state of mind. Substantial research has continually poured into this new area. As games continue to be imagined, created, and consumed, researchers and parents worry about the possible effects video gamers incur, while other researchers explore what video games have to offer. While some researchers have suggested an observational effect on the video gamer creating aggression and aggressive tendencies for those who play, there is not much evidence for this conclusion at this point (Ferguson, 2007; 2013). Others still suggest playing video games can be cathartic, or provide psychological relief through the expression of characters, actions within the video games, and strong emotions (Granic et al, 2014). And yet, others are discussing video games and internet play as unhealthy, socially deviant, and addictive while others discuss the importance of flow and immersion from the video game and virtual worlds; of what can be accomplished, felt, and experienced through the virtual worlds (Huesmann; 2007; Vasterling et al., 1993).

While these ideas are important to explore further, they appear to only touch the surface of what video games can offer to people. This is mainly because of the conception of this research being strongly based upon observational research with little distinction between behavior and intrapsychic processes, or cognitions, conscientiousness, parental upbringing, predisposition to aggression, engagement with others, and more. There is little discussion about the internal makeup of video gamers and how they view the games themselves. As a result, we know very little about the psychological temperament of a video gamer, yet we all are part of this experience in some fashion. In fact, common definitions and terminology of the constitution of a video gamer are primarily socially constructed and furthered by media, but based off of speculation and thoughts with no datum as proof. In essence, opinions have been taken as mainstream fact, without any concrete evidence to back these sentiments or views. Furthermore, this constitutes to self-confirmation bias by the media only presenting video gamers in one fashion: socially deviant from the rest of the populace. In return, the general population then internalizes these stereotypes and further uses the biased and unfounded terminology to discuss their lives or lives of people they know. It turns into a vicious cycle all created off of information that has very little or no proof behind it. Ironically, with the explosion of video games across multiple platforms (e.g. smart phones, tablets, consoles, computers, etc.) everyone these days could be considered a video gamer.

What talk or discussion is there of the relational experience gamers can have with their characters, their in-game experience, and conclusions they draw from playing the video game itself? Very little, at best, I am afraid. In fact, in an observational approach, which is what a good portion of the data is comprised of, we do not ask these questions, but primarily discuss the problematic use of gaming, lack of "real world relationships," and superficially condemn the video gamer population. This in turn has created stereotypes of what a video gamer may be like, someone living with his/her parents in their basement, another individual who may end up attacking an educational institution, while others still are considered to be losers, misanthropes, schizoid, having Asperger's, or socially deviant (Kowert, 2016). As humans are social creatures and rely upon social identity, video gamers have begun to cognitively think and believe their gaming habits are socially deviant even when they are not. This in turn reflects opinions which may not constitute actual feelings of the video gamers themselves!

However, with some reflexivity, attempting to view how your opinions and experiences bias your viewpoint or results, this error can be adjusted and sometimes completely fixed to a degree where the bias will not influence the research results. Most researchers do not stop and take time to see this, believing their research is immune to it, but as it is inherent in that we study what we are interested in, it is difficult to say we do not begin or complete research without believing a certain effect already exists.

While this book does not offer purely statistical evidence in a confirmation or statement of fact, it provides a different view of virtual worlds and a possible unconscious impact of playing them. More specifically, it addresses the research found within video games, attempting to bring the current research together to provide factual data upon the contentious topic.

It is important not to condemn the playing of video games based on rating, time spent, or games played, but to see through the playing into what the player is experiencing or the video gamer's experience of the virtualized world. This may require an observer to participate in the virtual world in order to fully comprehend its abilities, draws, and engagement. It is my suggestion that we should not be as concerned with the action itself (i.e. playing the video game), but the relationship between the video game and the person playing it. Play itself is not inherently negative or bad as some individuals suggest, but it allows the creativity of the individual to shine through with utilization of imagination.

This is just one of the possibilities and examples of "seeing through" the behavioral actions psychology sometimes gets caught up with. By conducting ourselves in this manner, it allows a deeper and more meaningful understanding to unfold about the game played, character or avatar chosen, and the person playing. However, in order to view the video gamer's experience, one must be familiar with the culture and the specific video game played. This generally means having more than a cursory glance of information about the video game and the created world. As a psychologist, I would not pretend to know how to conduct neurological surgery or make assumptions about the procedures used to conduct the surgery; because I am not trained or completely familiar with the topic. This is what current mental health professionals are resorting to with regard to video games, possibly because they do not understand or take the time to research deeper into the topic. In order to talk about a subject proficiently, an individual must understand the nature of the characters or avatars being played, have a sense of the storyline, meaning, and/or play of the video game, and be open to asking about a video gamer's experience while playing specific video games.

I do want to be clear, I am a doctor and psychologist first and a video gamer second. I grew up playing video games my entire life and wholly believe there are emotional experiences to be found, lessons learned, and lives lived within each video game. I use them in my therapy with clients, where discussing emerging themes and characters played to great success. I have used them in bringing families closer together and rekindling family structure. Furthermore, I have worked with video gamers on relationships through video gaming and how they interact, share their inner-most secrets, and generally behave in different contexts. I am surely called a "pro-gamer" and "sympathizer" for the video game industry. Again, these are just labels thrown around similar to the stereotypes we have for the video gamer population. I leave them behind and willingly acknowledge I am viewing this topic as a *psychologically minded video gamer*. I truly believe in order to understand the virtual worlds, expansive universes, and reasons why we play video games, you need to step into the arena and virtual worlds to experience what they can do and personally mean for you.

This is not to say everyone should play video games and they are what we need to solely focus on. However, if someone is going to conduct research, talk about, or conduct therapy with individuals who play video games, one should at least be familiar with the topic past a mainstream idea found so prevalent in our society today. By familiar I mean having actually played the game, watched it on a YouTube video, or at least be open minded to what video games can offer. Obviously playing the video game will give the best indication of the engagement one may feel when playing within the virtual realm, but with other means of exploration of the virtual realms at least some indication can be gathered from watching. Although, case examples and theoretical orientations will be brought forth later in the book as examples of using video games, their characters, and the gamer his or herself in therapeutic and/or family manners.

The format of this book is to offer a general idea of video game research. The following chapters will provide in-depth detail on the subjects covered and will try to be as comprehensive in nature as possible due to the expansive and ever changing nature of research. As such, one should always look to the people mentioned, the research discussed, and continue researching the areas of interest as everything known or researched will not be able to be covered. Use your own judgment and insight on the topical research, and enjoy the book's content and journey. The research mentioned and discussed is specifically chosen as the authors sited are leaders and experts in the field.

The chapters are broken up into the different areas as they are important and diverse topics being handled through mainstream research and media, therefore providing increasing relevance to the general research population. Topics will include video game addiction, immersion, personalities of the video gamer, video games as meaningful and emotional experiences, the changing genre field, archetypes of video games, therapeutic implications, and much more.

This book should be considered a starting point in understanding the video gamer on a more sophisticated level. It is not an endpoint of the knowledge in the field, although it will give the reader more than basic information of the video gamer. It is an attempt at being a doorway into the realm of the video gamers from a different point of assessment, based on their experience of the different and various video game worlds and characters available. Instead of primarily looking at video gamers as a different societal entity, I believe it to be of high importance to discuss the experience of the game itself. It should make the reader think differently about the topic. What brings video gamers to that specific game? Why do they like one video game franchise over another? What characters do they like to play more? Is there a specific genre they prefer over others? Why one genre over another? What keeps them coming back to the video game and playing? Do they like to play with others or prefer exploring a video game's world alone? Why did they choose one action over another? Is there a story behind their character? These are just some of the questions we should be asking in an attempt to understand the experience video games can provide us. Let us begin with an overview of what video games are.

References

Aarseth, E., Bean, A. M., Boonen, H., Carras, M. C., Coulson, M., Das, D., . . . Van Rooij, A. J. (2016). Scholars' Open Debate paper on the World Health Organization ICD-11 Gaming Disorder proposal. *Journal of Behavioral Addictions, 6*(3), 267–270.

American Psychiatric Association (APA). (2013). *Diagnostic and statistical manual of mental disorders: DSM-5*. Washington, DC: American Psychiatric Association.

Anderson, C. A., & Bushman, B. J. (2001). Effects of violent video games on aggressive behavior, aggressive cognition, aggressive affect, physiological arousal, and prosocial behavior: A meta-analytic review of the scientific literature. *Psychological Science, 12*(5), 353–359.

Anderson, C. A., & Dill, K. E. (2000). Video games and aggressive thoughts, feelings, and behavior in the laboratory and in life. *Journal of Personality and Social Psychology, 78*(4), 772–790.

Bean, A. M., Nielsen, R. K. L., van Rooij, A. J., & Ferguson, C. J. (2017). Video game addiction: The push to pathologize video games. *Professional Psychology: Research and Practice*. Advance online publication. http://dx.doi.org/10.1037/pro0000150.

Dill, K. E., & Dill, J. C. (1998). Video game violence: A review of the empirical literature. *Aggression and Violent Behavior, 3*(4), 407–428.

Ferguson, C. J. (2007). Evidence for publication bias in video game violence affects literature: A meta-analytic review. *Aggression and Violent Behavior, 12*, 470–482.

Ferguson, C. J. (2013). Violent video games and the Supreme Court: Lesson for the scientific community in the wake of the Brown v. Entertainment Merchants Association. *American Psychologist, 68*, 57–74. doi: 10.1037/a0030597.

Granic, I., Lobel, A., & Engels, R. C. M. E. (2014). The benefits of playing video games. *American Psychologist, 69*(1), 66–78.

Huesmann, L. R. (2007). The impact of electronic media violence: Scientific theory and research. *Journal of Adolescent Health, 41*(6), S6–S13.

Kowert, R. (2016). *A parent's guide to video games: The essential guide to understanding how video games impact your child's physical, social, and psychological well-being.* Online: CreateSpace.

Vasterling, J., Jenkins, R. A., Tope, D. M., & Burish, T. G. (1993). Cognitive distraction and relaxation training for the control of side effects due to cancer chemotherapy. *Journal of Behavioral Medicine, 16*, 65–79.

World Health Organization (WHO). (2016a). Gaming disorder proposal. Retrieved from http://apps.who.int/classifications/icd11/browse/proposals/l-m/en#/http://id.who.int/icd/entity/1602669465?readOnlytrue&actionAddNewEntityProposal&stableProposalGroupId47bfdbcd-524a-4af7a179-02f29517f23a

World Health Organization (WHO). (2016b). Hazardous gaming proposal. Retrieved from http://apps.who.int/classifications/icd11/browse/proposals/ l-m/en#/http://id.who.int/icd/entity/1602669465?readOnlytrue&actionAddNewEntityProposal&stableProposalGroupId93aeefc3-b9e2-43b7abd1-2ca742d70a79

What Are Video Games?

2

Since their inception in the mid-1900s, video games have become a part of our culture. They have come exceptionally far in conceptual ideas, platform abilities, storylines, and social interactions due to significant advancements in technology and increase in players. From the beginning of Pong in the 1970s with simplistic vertical movement controls (akin to two-dimensional tennis or ping pong) to the more advanced Xbox, Playstation, and Nintendo systems of today, much has evolved and changed (Kent, 2001). With a recent governmental article suggesting over 97% of youth play a form of video games, whether it be on their phone, home based console, or computer, it is clear this form of virtual enjoyment is here to stay (Lenhart et al., 2008). Gender gaps in video games have additionally diminished over the years with most researchers and scholars agreeing that both men and women make up equal portions of the player base (ESA, 2017; Romano, 2014). What's more, a new development of video games have recently come forth: virtual reality. Virtual reality focuses on a deeper immersive experience, furthering what is already created by normal video games through the use of more senses, in order to process what is being seen, felt, or heard.

For example, playing a video game on a television screen has an immersive experience to it, but the space between the person, controller, video game system, avatar player, and surrounding world can easily pull the player out of the immersion under the right circumstances. With virtual reality, there is no conception of the space between the game and the player because all other "noise" has been taken away by the virtual reality controllers. There is no space between the player and the game any longer as the player is usually playing through a perspective similar to the character's eyes. Experiencing the virtual world as another entity not akin of our world is remarkable to the individual undergoing it. It drives us to move further into the world, explore, and draw conclusions from the surrounding landscapes, rooms, worlds, or puzzles.

Until virtual reality becomes more readily available and hosts a much greater breadth of game choices, it is still considered a new area of video game play. As a direct result, it is difficult to provide much research in this area as the topic is still in the neonate stage of existence. Furthermore, while immersion occurs more easily with virtual reality, it still arises in current video game play, possibly to a similar extent. In order to understand video games in their current form of today, it is important to provide basic information about video games, playability, characters, and different and important topics.

A Brief Overview

A video game can be considered anything that requires human interaction with a user interface or program generating visual feedback. These user or player interfaces are generally keyboards or controllers of a sort that allow movement within the virtual reality landscape. The virtual reality is projected onto a screen of various sizes and can produce two or three-dimensional avatars (Meadows, 2007). The individual playing the game will have to complete tasks in the virtual world or fight bosses on various scales of difficulty. By accomplishing these tasks, the player is allowed further access to storyline, levels, equipment, and characters. The overall goal is to continue on within the storyline and discover the world further as the individual is playing. Usually, the player gains a sense of accomplishment from playing the game and finishing tasks, quests, and objectives.

The beginning of the game is where rudimentary skills are taught and learned, impressions of the game are acknowledged, and the rules are enforced. The player proceeds through the beginning stages of the game to gain elementary concepts taught by the virtual world through mini tutorials. They are unknowingly taught by the program to the player through instructions, mini quests, and quick and simple directions. Most of the time, the world being played will explain the existence of the world through these instructions in an attempt to mask the directions, controls, and instructions to the player. With most video game players, these first few hours in the game are what can be considered "make or break" gameplay where the player acclimatises to the world, controls, and experiences the gameplay determining whether they will continue until completion, work slowly, or even discontinue the game itself after the small introduction to it.

Video gamers play on multiple systems usually preferring a specific system due to games, graphics, and playability. Each individual video game system manufacturer and brand has a unique controller with which to manipulate the environments. As the "war of the systems" (Nintendo, Sony, Microsoft, and Sega (Sega is no longer a manufacturer of systems, but a producer of video games; McFerran, 2012) began each system had their own adaptions to the controllers. However, as technology has continued further, the controls have additionally expanded to have multiple buttons and abilities associated with each button, controls requiring human movement, and some slight uniqueness to each system's controller, with Nintendo continually pushing the envelope with innovative ideas and the other manufacturers following suit, expanding their own uniqueness in the process (Ciolek, 2014). This console war continues and has given birth to the world of the computer gamer. Through the development of cheaper technology creation, gamers now have the access and ability to build their own video game computer system and consoles to their own specifications.

Developing and Playing a Character

Character development can be seen as an attribute which the video gamer can usually control within most video games. They can choose which elements of the avatar's personal abilities they wish to pursue through talent choices as they level through the video game. Eventually deciding which elements they can ultimately have gets tougher, when there are what video gamers call "deep talent trees." Examples include: World of Warcraft with a choice of three different abilities and a new set unlocking every 15 levels (Blizzard Entertainment, 2017), Commander Shepard in the Mass Effect series with his individual abilities dependent upon his specialization (Bioware, 2007), and Fallout characters in the beginning choices of the game (i.e. luck, skill, weapons; Interplay Entertainment, 1997, Bethesda Game Studios, 1997). Luckily, within most video games there are options to change the talents out for new ones or a better playability factor, but the cost to do so is usually quite high requiring in game monetary systems in order to complete the change. Most video gamers usually focus on the abilities which allow them to produce the most damage, healing, and survivability. Therefore there are always talents which are seen as "inept, minimal," or "not worthy" being rarely chosen except for the scarcest circumstances. Usually, due to the lack of usefulness of the attributes and talents game creators and crafters will "rebalance" a class, talent, or tree in order to make an attempt at focusing the player to use the rarely used characteristic. Most of the time it makes another talent undesirable and the cycle repeats itself.

The decisions of specific talents are usually opinion and mathematically based by players who commonly and primarily play in the method called PvE or Player Versus Environment (also known as Game Theory). A majority of video games have this playability system in place, allowing the player to advance through the game using the talents chosen alone or with company in a group, to quest through different zones to level up. Players interact with Artificial Intelligence (AI), Non-Player Characters (NPCs) and/or human companions in order to start or complete a quest or storyline scenario. The video games focus on this play style because it allows them to advance through the video game and have a basis for their decisions, which impact the playability of their avatars. Furthermore, PvE modes in video games usually have a deeper focus on quests and the storyline; the gamer become more immersed as the player progresses through missions and challenges. An example of this is best illustrated by MMOs such as Guild Wars or World of Warcraft, where in-game cut-scenes are initiated by the player completing specific quests or quest chains (Arenanet, 2017; Blizzard Entertainment, 2017). Without the progression of the video game in this manner the video gamer will have difficulties experiencing how the storyline progresses. MMOs additionally have another aspect to their nature called "dailies", or repeatable quests which enhance the possibility of the player replaying a specific area of the video game or gaining influence, or more commonly noted as reputation, with a faction who is offering the quest.

There are also other methods and manners to play video games which are not as prominent as PvE, but are played nevertheless, and have a significant amount of players. Another comparable play style similar to PvE is PvP or Player versus Player. In this style of play, the main objective is to skirmish against other players in the video game virtual space in an attempt to determine who is the better competitor. It is an interactive multiplayer interface, focusing on battles and conflict in the video game between two or more live participants. Society has seen a burst of interest in this play area due to tournaments becoming more available for viewing via live streaming, with the favored streaming service called Twitch. Blizzard Entertainment (2017) and Riot Games (2017), prominent video game creators, hold tournaments throughout the year focusing on this type of play, pitting video game players against one another with the winner gathering thousands of dollars for their video game combat skills. This play style's fame has continued to grow in more recent years, resulting in massive audiences cheering across the globe while millions of other hopeful video gamers watch the competition through online streaming. This further spurned many high school and college students to play the same games in hopes of being able to attain a similar status and be invited to the "holy grail" competitions. The video gamer focuses on talents which allow high damage and survivability, but in an attempt to overrun, "Zerg" rush, or destroy their opponent when playing one versus one. However, there is also team play which can consist of anywhere from two to ten players on one team against another team made up of the same number of opponents. These talents or characters played may seem similar to the PvE selections, but the choice changes depending upon the opponent the other video gamer uses, rather than just needing to be more powerful than the AI computer, usually resulting in varying rotations of talent and character choices.

The last main playstyle is a rather unique one, much smaller in population, but still fairly popular as a play style: RP or Roleplaying. These types of players are primarily found in MMOs (Massively Multiplayer Online) as the type of the videogame allows the player to roam the area and pretend to be their character in the virtual world. These players focus on the playing of their character enacting a real-life persona in the world with a backstory, employment, and even specific clothing. The video gamers become their avatars while playing in the virtual world and assume the character's role while playing. It is similar to how an actor plays a part in a play or movie, the video gamer develops the character and acts out the character's role. Role-playing can be enacted online in the form of groups ranging from two to hundreds of avatars. The worlds, backstories, and characters may last for hours to years, depending on the richness of the story and the tenacity of the involved players. Through this individual and group acting, the video gamers collaboratively create stories. The stories are based upon the characterization, actions, and responses of the avatar. Generally, there are rules and guidelines which are used to govern the interactions appropriately, but with respect to the rules, the video gamers may improvise freely and allow their choices to shape the flow and context of the created narrative. Regardless of the choice in play, all video games have immersive aspects within the different styles of play, making them impressively important to discuss in the clinical experience.

Understanding the Point of View

Perspective of video games being played greatly enhances and informs the manner in which the video game will be played. There are multiple different perspectives to be had, but there are specific ones which are used more often. For instance, the primary perspectives used in today's video games rely on one of five perspectives: top down, side scrolling, 1st person, 2nd person, and 3rd person. Top down and side scrolling are considered to be two dimensional (2D) perceptions while 1st person, 2nd person, and 3rd person are three-dimensional (3D) viewpoints (Meadows, 2007).

Two dimensional perspectives rely on programming movement conceptions similar to a flips books. The character moves left or right and as they move the programmer has created a new picture for each movement which gives the illusion that the character is seamlessly moving. However the character's movement generally are only comprised of two to six different images. Three dimensional perspectives are comprised of building a virtual doll and incorporating more complex movements in order to achieve the fluidity of running, walking, fighting, etc. This perspective requires much more incorporation of movements and programming due to the complexity of the perspective, buildout of the avatar, and range of movements.

Each perspective has its own pros and cons such as the need for limited graphics, repeated use of some graphics, camera angles, and complexity. As the perspective increase from 2D to 3D the complexity of the video game increases significantly. It is also important to note that newer video games have been able to incorporate multiple perspectives and the ability to switch between them at the click of a button on a keyboard or controller.

Table 2.1 Video Game Perspectives

Perspective	Type	Video game Examples
2D Perspectives	Top Down	Sim City, Railroad Tycoon, The Legend of Zelda (NES), Pokemon
	Side Scrolling	MegaMan, Double Dragon, Sonic, Super Mario Brothers
3D Perspectives	1st Person	Doom, Quake, Flight Simulators
	2nd Person	Resident Evil, The Legend of Zelda (N64), Final Fantasy
	3rd Person	Tomb Raider, Super Mario 64, World of Warcraft

Adapted from Meadows (2007).

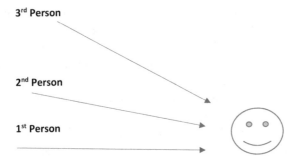

Figure 2.1 Video Game Perspectives
Adapted from Meadows (2007)

The top down perspective is also referred to a "bird's-eye-view" where the player sees the game from the camera angle of directly above the avatar. The side-scrolling games is when the viewpoint is taken from the side and the avatar runs from the left to the right to complete the levels. 1st person perspective video games are rendered from the viewpoint of the character being played as if you were looking through the character's eyes. 2nd person perspective is similar to 1st, but the camera is elevated and behind the avatar allowing the video game player to see the back of the avatar. Finally, 3rd person perspective is even more elevated than 2nd perspective and the player can see the entire body of the avatar and surrounding features (Meadows, 2007).

Dimensionally different perspectives offer different points of view and frame in which to experience and play the video game. By zooming in close one can see the fine detail put into place within the video game while zooming out provides a different perspective of the overwhelming expansiveness of the virtual world. Each playstyle makes it easier and harder to play a video game depending whether a player wants to micro manage or play from a god-like perspective.

Ludology

Ludology is derived from the Latin word of "ludus" which has several meanings like "play, game, sport," and "training." Historically, the term has been used to describe the study of games in general and has far reaching interdisciplinary actions. For instance, it is used in anthropology, psychology, communication studies, sociology, and teaching/learning to learn more about the systematic concept of how and why we play games currently and historically (Caillois, 1961; Egenfeldt-Nielsen et al., 2016).

The concept of Ludology has been in existence for a very long time. It is considered to be interdisciplinary and is the study of games, the act of playing them, the players, and the culture surrounding the game. Ludology is not just about video games, as how the concept will be primarily used in this capacity for this book, but all games that have even been created from the existence of sticks and stones to marbles to board games to sports to video games. Every game has a set amount of rules and regulations which require adherence to in order to be victorious. If the rules are not followed, then the game is not a game any longer. In essence, the rules are what create the game and the primarily components, along with the reactions of the players, of being studied in the framework of Ludology.

Primary theorists and researchers which Ludology utilizes as a theoretical basis for studying the area stem from Johan Huizinga (1971) and Roger Caillois (1961). These two perspectives are used due to the studying of various types of play and games within society. Huzinga (1971) began with the attempt to explain video games through the conceptual lens of competitiveness. Caillois (1961; Kapp, 2012) expanded upon this concept and created a taxonomy comprised of four play categories organizing diverse games, play styles, and player types. This leads many researchers to use these forms of play to study the concept of video games.

Researchers studying the concept of ludology generally ask the question, "What do games do to people?" They conduct studies and research using surveys, controlled laboratory experiments, and ethnography in order to gain more insight into the field. There are numerous studies which discuss the importance, the danger, and the benefits of video games in this approach —much more than what can be explained in this book, but Chapter Five includes much of the current research and societal thinking of video games and the effects upon the player.

Sociologically informed research has begun to move away from the simplistic idea of whether video games are "good" or "bad" due to the simpleminded manner in which research has been conducted using these approaches. Instead, this area of research seeks to understand the role and complexity in which individuals play video games (Crawford, 2012). An example of this would be Sherry Turkle's (1994) research exploring participation in online multiplayer games in order to examine personal issues of identity.

Research focusing on other parts of video game play have shown other important aspects of video gamer personality development: video gamers have been shown to have appropriately developing personalities, similar to individuals who do not play video games (Bean & Groth-Marnat, 2014; Bean, 2015; Bean et al., 2016). In some cases, research has shown video gamers have lower levels of emotionality in stressful situations, suggesting gamers may manage stress better than non-gamers (Ferguson & Rueda, 2010). This is further consistent with claims of researchers suggesting video games may be considered to be providing a safe haven for individuals to experience and process emotional content (Jansz, 2005).

Durkin and Barber (2002) found no support for the stereotypical negative beliefs about computer video games and concluded that: "computer [video] game play is not necessarily a monolithic, moronic, or antisocial imposition on children's lives" (p. 375). Contrary to popular beliefs about digital games this study found that among a sample of 1,304 American students, playing video games correlated with positive adolescent development. Compared to adolescents that did not play computer games, gamers reported lower levels of depressed mood, lower levels of substance abuse, lower levels of absenteeism from school, lower levels of risky behavior and disobedience, higher levels of family closeness, higher levels of active engagement in clubs, and finally they exhibited higher grade point averages.

Other evidence has suggested that video games are related to increased social interactions of individuals who suffer from difficulties with social engagement along with increasing curricular engagement (Adachi & Willoughby, 2013; Durkin, 2010; Nebel, Schneider, & Rey, 2016; Shute, Ventura, & Ke, 2014). For instance, games like Minecraft may be valuable in promoting social engagement for individuals on the Autism Spectrum (Ringland, Wolf, Faucett, Dombrowski, & Hayes, 2016). Related to this, research suggests that social game playing is related to promotion of prosocial behaviors, social engagement and empowerment, and problem solving skills (Adachi & Willoughby, 2013; Nebel et al., 2016; Shute et al., 2014).

Meaningful and Emotional Experiences

Video games are often stereotyped as pure entertainment without any beneficial remunerations. They are generally seen as "wastes of time" and only played by individuals who are considered to be stereotypical lonely, overweight, underachievers, introverted, lazy, and socially inept even with research stating otherwise (Kowert, Festl, & Quandt, 2014). However, these ideological fallacies have primarily been purported by researchers, clinicians, policy makers, and politicians of older generations who did not grow up with video games as rampantly played as they are today (Ferguson, 2015). While older age cohorts are typically harsher on their conceptualization of video games and video gamers, younger researchers and players tend to be more lenient and accepting of the medium.

Video games have been able to elicit meaningful and emotional content via their immersive storylines and the by-product of playing. They have been shown to be a safe place for video gamers to experience different forms of reality and play gratifying contextual experiences and demands placed upon them. Furthermore, video games have been shown to be especially important for adolescents who are in the midst of constructing an identity or experiencing an identity crisis (Janz, 2005). Jonathan Frome (2007) purported that by playing video games the player enacts an observer-participant role. In this role the video gamer will engage with the material form of the video game, but not change it. They are merely engaging with the video game as a player and observing their interactions with the game. It is considered to be akin with watching a movie, the individual is watching the video game and its linear storyline unfold as they progress through the narrative. This is where streaming services have been able to use people's interest in watching others play video games to their benefit. Twitch allows players to stream their video game play for the benefit of having others watch them and enjoy the emotional experience through an observer stance of not just the video game, but the video gamer as well.

The other role Frome (2007) discusses is the actor-participant which is when the video gamers change the actual landscape of the video game due to their influence. For instance, in World of Warcraft, the players advance through the storyline and when they complete a section of the map or world, the landscape changes. Another example would be in playing Gears of War or Halo. When players push a button to fire their weapons or throw grenades, the effect is lasting upon the virtual realm, usually by a bullet hole or a mark upon where the grenade detonated. No matter what occurs afterwards, the virtual world remains changed forever within that saved game. The video gamer can also change the landscape by progressing through the game and unlocking new areas or by physically changing them.

Both manners in which players interact with the video game induce emotional experiences. However, they are diversely created. For instance, within the role of the observer-participant, the observer's emotional reactions are based upon what they see, hear, and intrinsically feel. Their interpretation of the events does not change based upon their playing, but what they observe only. Therefore as Frome (2007) suggests, the player cannot change the inputs in order to change their emotional responses. For the actor-participant player, this changes as they have direct control of the play. Therefore their emotional responses are based upon what they enact or do within the video game rather than only what they perceive.

Jaime Banks (2015) additionally suggest that players relate to their avatars in meaningful and emotional capacities. She suggests that there are different ways in which one can relate to their online persona through patterns of self-differentiation, emotional intimacy, and perceived agency. Banks builds upon previous researchers' claims of humans engaging and making connections with online avatars through a bilateral social relationship (Boler, 2007; Lewis et al., 2008; Nowak & Rauh, 2005; Reeves & Nass, 1996; Allucquère, 2001; Turkle, 2014). Through further examination of player and their avatars, Banks (2015) reports that some video games relate to their avatars as real social others. In essence, video gamers create meaningful and emotional connections to their created avatars as they would of human being and non-virtual world relationships. Through the playing of these avatars and the programmed narratives and challenges, facilitation of emotional relationships develop between players and their characters (Gaider, 2013; Posey, 2013).

Through these perceptions the video gamer creates emotional and meaningful experiences. They are generated, not just by the game itself, but by the player's interaction with the medium. The narrative aspect of the video game is a large and important measure as the storytelling of the video game can lead one to grow closer with their characters. With the inception of character development and creation, the video game player can additionally immerse themselves in another manner to create their emotional connection to the video game. Furthermore, developers have additionally been attempting to create more video games that focus upon the story of the characters to impart a tale or experience one may endure. This form of emotionally relating to the video games has become more popular over the last decade.

Heavy Rain is a prime example of telling an emotional story which grasps the video game player. Heavy Rain tells the story of a father, whom the player plays as, attempting to save his son from becoming a victim of a serial killer within the game. The player is tasked with stopping the killing and immersed into the experience of possibly losing their own son. Through the trials found within the game the player has to make moral decisions in order to attempt to save his son, which includes conducting reckless acts and possibly harming himself and/or others. Even though this is a fictional and virtual game, the emotions created by the player become real and exhaustive placing a toll on the video gamer.

Heavy Rain is not the only game that uses emotional experiences to tap into the human psyche. Papo & Yo is about a boy who is followed by a monster who is helpful at times, but also attempts to attack and harm him during other encounters. The boy must endure the happenstances where the monster attacks him and hide and escape efficiently to progress through the game. Unknown to new players of Papo & Yo, the monster is symbolic for his alcoholic father and the need to hide from him when he is drunk and abusive.

That Dragon, Cancer is another well-known video game where a video game developer immortalized his son's battle with cancer. The player must advance through the game and care for the infant son who was diagnosed at the age of 12 months and given only a short time to live. The game is designed to give the player the high and low periods the programmer experienced through the loss of his own son due to cancer. The game was praised for being an emotional experience from a parent's point of view, forcing the player to deal with the intense emotional events of losing a child to forces beyond their control, no matter the decisions made.

These examples are the ones which influence the player through deep emotional connections. They are extreme examples, but confer the emotionality the player must face and endure in order to complete the game. Other video games may not induce these deep emotional events, but still incur an emotional experience from playing them. Oliver and Raney (2011) coined the term "Eudaimonia" to refer to "gratifications associated with meaningful entertainment" (Oliver et al, 2015, pg 3). They further stipulated that "eudaimonic gratifications tend to be associated with appreciation of the understanding and insight concerning meaning-in-life questions and issues regarding the human condition" (Oliver et al, 2015, pg 3). As a result, the video gaming industry has been embracing a more substantive humanistic approach to video game narratives, allowing a deeper and greater immersive and emotional connection to the narrative and characters played. As a result, video games have been able to elicit and impart emotional and meaningful experiences to the video game player.

Case in Point: Amy

Amy is a 15 year old girl who plays video games in order to reduce her tension and also interact with others. She reported that she does not feel safe and secure when talking with others in real life. She asserted symptoms of anxiety, tension, and panic attacks when she is forced to interact with other individuals in social situations. However, she prefers to play as different characters role playing with different "personas" in order to placate and make friends within the virtual realm. Her "personas" were different ages, gender roles, and family roles. Depending on which one she played as, she was a different character and interacted differently. Amy had multiple friends within the video game which she felt accepted by even though she was playing as a different personified avatar when interacting with them.

Amy had about 15 different characters she preferred to play as within the game Minecraft. She would prefer to be a different character depending on the situation within the game and whom she was playing with. For instance, with a boy her age she was an older sister who had to take care of the boy as they had lost their parents in a tragic accident. For another character, she was one of 12 individuals who had created their own tribe and were attempting to resettle their people into a new area within the game. Furthermore, on another character, she was a resource for another individual committing crimes and other atrocities in the name of the warlord. It is easy to say her characters were quite diverse.

Amy would talk about her characters in a loving manner focusing on aspects she enjoyed and other ones she did not. However, she had built up deep histories and backgrounds for all of her characters and the various reasons they were acting in different manners. She would talk fondly of them and even relate some of her real life experiences to theirs (no she was not killing anyone). She even still had both of her parents, but would tend to play as the orphan character more when she was feeling estranged from them or guilty because she knew she had done something to gain their disappointment. At other times when she was happy, she would play as different characters and focus upon helping others or guiding them through the game on quests.

She created these characters to help regulate her moods and process her emotional experiences in the real world through the rich narratives and backstories. Her avatars had meaning for her, not just as playable characters, but as individuals who represented a part of her, but most of all who helped her relate to other people. Without video games, she would have lacked an emotional outlet, an ability to process difficult emotions, and a way relate to others. She was able to use both Frome's (2007) ideas of the actor-observer and the actor-participant to help her regulate her emotional content while safely relating to other individuals on her terms.

As Amy's case demonstrates, emotional video games have an important place in the world, but so do the meaningfulness and emotions which video gamers create with their playing and character development. These interactions, experiences, emotions, avatars, and choices made within the game are important to discuss with video gamers, as they hold a wealth of information about the video gamers and their individual psyches.

References

Adachi, P. J. C., & Willoughby, T. (2013). More than just fun and games: The longitudinal relationships between strategic video games, self-reported problem solving skills, and academic grades. *Journal of Youth and Adolescence, 42*(7), 1041–1052. https://doi.org/10.1007/s10964-013-9913-9.

Allucque_re, R. S. (2001). *The war of desire and technology at the close of the mechanical age.* Cambridge, MA: MIT Press.

ArenaNet. (2017). Guild Wars Wiki. Retrieved from wiki.guildwars.com/wiki/Main_Page.

Banks, J. (2015). Object, me, symbiote, other: A social typology of player–avatar relationships. *First Monday, 20,* 2.

Bean, A., & Groth-Marnat, G. (2014). Video gamers and personality: A five-factor model to understand game playing style. *Psychology of Popular Media Culture, 5*(1), 27–38. https://doi.org/10.1037/ppm0000025

Bean, A. M. (2015). Video gamers' personas: A five factor study exploring personality elements of the video gamer [Doctoral Thesis]. Pacifica Graduate Institute.

Bean, A. M., Ferro, L. S., Vissoci, J. R. N., Rivero, T., Groth-marnat, G., Dafter, R., . . . Reader, E. (2016). The emerging adolescent World of Warcraft video gamer: A five factor exploratory profile model. *Entertainment Computing, 5*(17), 45–54. https://doi.org/10.1016/j.entcom.2016.08.006.

Bethesda Game Studios (1997). Fallout.

Bioware. (2007). Mass Effect.

Blizzard Entertainment. (2017.) New player's guide. Retrieved from https://worldofwarcraft.com/en-us/game/new-players-guide.

Boler, M. (2007). Hypes, hopes and actualities: New digital Cartesianism and bodies in cyberspace. *New Media & Society, 9*(1), pp. 139–168.

Caillois, R. (1961). *Man, play, and games.* Champaign, IL: University of Illinois Press.

Ciolek, T. (2014). 11 gaming innovations we owe to Nintendo. Retrieved from www.ign.com/articles/2014/08/26/11-gaming-innovations-we-owe-to-nintendo.

Crawford, G. (2012). *Video gamers.* London: Routledge.

Durkin, K. (2010). Videogames and young people with developmental disorders. *Review of General Psychology, 14*(2), 122–140. https://doi.org/10.1037/a0019438.

Durkin, K., & Barber, B. (2002). Not so doomed: computer game play and positive adolescent development. *Journal of Applied Developmental Psychology, 23*(4), 373–392. https://doi.org/10.1016/S0193-3973(02)00124-7.

Egenfeldt-Nielsen, S., Smith, J. H., & Tosca, S. P. (2016). Understanding video games: The essential introduction. New York: Routledge.

Entertainment Software Association (ESA). (2017). Essential facts about the computer and video game industry. Retrieved from www.theesa.com/wp-content/uploads/2017/06/!EF2017_Design_FinalDigital.pdf.

Ferguson, C. J., & Rueda, S. M. (2010). The Hitman study: Violent video game exposure effects on aggressive behavior, hostile feelings, and depression. *European Psychologist, 15*(2), 99–108. https://doi.org/10.1027/1016-9040/a000010

Ferguson, C. J. (2015). Clinicians' attitudes toward video games vary as a function of age, gender and negative beliefs about youth: A sociology of media research approach. *Computers in Human Behavior, 52,* 379–386. https://doi.org/10.1016/j.chb.2015.06.016

Frome, J. (2007). Eight ways videogames generate emotion. In Proceedings of DiGRA, 2007.

Gaider, D. (2013). Sex in video games. Presentation at Game Developers Conference 2013. Retrived at www.gdcvault.com/play/1017796/Sex-in-Video.

Huizinga, J. (1971). *Homo ludens: A study of the play element in culture.* Boston, MA: Beacon Press.

Interplay Entertainment. (1997). Fallout.

Jansz, J. (2005). The emotional appeal of violent video games for adolescent males. *Communication Theory, 15*(3), 219–241.

Kapp, K. M. (2012). The gamification of learning and instruction: Game-based methods and strategies for training and education. San Francisco, CA: Pfeiffer.

Kent, S. (2001). "And then there was Pong". Ultimate history of video games. New York: Three Rivers Press.

Kowert, R., Festl, R., & Quandt, T. (2014). Unpopular, overweight, and socially inept: reconsidering the stereotype of online gamers. *Cyberpsychology, Behavior and Social Networking, 17*(3), 141–146. https://doi.org/10.1089/cyber.2013.0118.

Lenhart, A., Kahne, J., Middaugh, E., Rankin Macgill, A., Evans, C., & Vitak, J. (2008). *Teens, video games, and civics: Teens' gaming experiences are diverse and include significant social interaction and civic engagement.* Washington, DC: Pew Internet & American Life Project.

Lewis, M. L., Weber, R., & Bowman, N. D. (2008). They may be pixels, but they're MY pixels: Developing a metric of character attachment in role-playing video games. *Cyberpsychology and Behavior, 11*(4), 515–518.

Meadows, M. S. (2007). *I, avatar: The culture and consequences of having a second life.* Indianapolis, IN: New Riders.

McFerran, D. (2012). The rise and fall of Sega Enterprises. Retrieved from www.eurogamer.net/articles/2012–02–22-the-rise-and-fall-of-sega-enterprises.

Nebel, S., Schneider, S., & Rey, G. D. (2016). Mining learning and crafting scientific experiments: A literature review on the use of Minecraft in education and research. *Educational Technology and Society, 19*(2), 355–366.

Nowak, K. L., & Rauh, C. (2005). The influence of the avatar on online perceptions of anthropomorphism, androgyny, credibility, homophily, and attraction. *Journal of Computer Mediated Communication Electronic Edition, 11*(1), 153–178.

Oliver, M. B., Bowman, N. D., Woolley, J. K., Rogers, R., Sherrick, B. I., & Chung, M.-Y. (2015). Video games as meaningful entertainment experiences. *Psychology of Popular Media Culture, 5*(4), 390–405.

Oliver, M. B., & Raney, A. A. (2011). Entertainment as pleasurable and meaningful: Identifying hedonic and eudaimonic motivations for entertainment consumption. *Journal of Communication, 61*, 984–1004. http://dx.doi.org/10.1111/j.1460-2466 .2011.01585.x

Posey, J. (2013). Tastes like chicken: Authenticity in a totally fake world. Retrieved at http://schedule2013.gdconf.com/session-id/823740. Presented at the Game Developers Conference, San Francisco, CA.

Reeves, B., & Nass, C. (1996). *The media equation: How people treat computers, television, and new media like real people and places.* Stanford, CA: CSLI Publ.

Ringland, K. E., Wolf, C. T., Faucett, H., Dombrowski, L., & Hayes, G. R. (2016). "Will I always be not social?": Re-Conceptualizing Sociality in the Context of a Minecraft Community for Autism. *Proceedings of the 2016 CHI Conference on Human Factors in Computing Systems—CHI '16,* (May), 1256–1269. https://doi.org/10.1145/2858036. 2858038.

Riot Games (2017). Riot Games. Retrieved from https://www.riotgames.com/.

Romano, A. (2014). "Adult women are now the largest demographic in gaming". *The Daily Dot*. Retrieved from www.dailydot.com/parsec/adult-women-largest-gaming-demographic/?fb=ss&prtnr=nerdist.

Shute, V., Ventura, M., & Ke, F. (2014). The power of play: The effects of Portal 2 and Lumosity on cognitive and noncognitive skills. *Computers & Education, 80*, 58–67. https://doi.org/10.1016/j.compedu.2014.08.013

Turkle, S. (1994). Constructions and reconstructions of self in virtual reality: Playing in the MUDs. *Mind, Culture, and Activity, 1*(3), 158–67.

Turkle, S. (2014). *Life on the screen: Identity in the age of the Internet.* New York: Simon & Schuster.

Video Game Genres   **3**

To entirely categorize video game genres is an insurmountable task to many. The evolution of the video gamer's experience and video game playability are constantly changing. When video games first appeared they were easily placed into categories comparable to books of different reading genres. As the medium has continued to expand, evolve, and more developers have emerged, video game genres have continued to increase. As a result, from four categories sprung eight, then sixteen, and so on, continually multiplying.

The snowballing and continual development of video games and genres has left researchers in a difficult predicament when they attempt to discuss and research the different video game genres (Apperley, 2006; Crawford, 1997; McAllister, 2013). In turn, an expansive realm of video game genres exists to this day with multiple subgenres consisting within each overarching genre. A subgenre results in a trickledown effect where the superseding genre (supergenre) is at the top of the pyramid and each subgenre falls below it. For example, playing a video game on your phone or tablet such as Clash of Clans or Farm Heroes Saga falls into the supergenre of Mobile games, and in turn specifically the subgenre of Freemium games, free to play, but usually having an option to pay with real money for electronic items (e-items) in order to progress further through the storyline or play.

Briefly looking closer at Clash of Clans (Supercell, 2012) and Farm Heroes Saga (King, 2016), it is easy to see they are completely different games even though they fall into the supergenre of Mobile games because of the method played. In Clash of Clans, the primary goals are to expand your territory and defend it through the use of troops created with resources and buildings created throughout the game. Usually it requires quicker waiting periods in the beginning extending through time and resources required for finishing building construction or upgrade as it progresses. The player additionally joins a "clan" with other individuals playing the game from their personal mobile devices forming a typical and similar bond seen through team approach games like football or soccer. In Farm Heroes Saga, the main goal is to collect farm items like strawberries, carrots, and apples by connecting at least three identical items together to disperse the line and gain boosts and points; similar to Tetris. There is no team play, clans, or guilds, although other players connected through the game's built in interface can help by clearing blockades and giving "lives" or additional chances to the player. If mobile games can vary this much within their genre, computer and video games systems are considered to be even more diverse. That small bit about each of these games gives a greater of the convoluted aspect of video game genres. With that in mind, let's dive into a brief history of video game genres.

History of Video Game Genres

A video game genre is set by the game play challenges, storyline, and game-world context found in the interactive world itself. The playing of the video game as determined by the developer (creators and architects of the video games) governs how it is to be psychically construed genre-wise. Viewing video games through the lens of genres illuminates common factors which bring them together whether it is game mechanics, social ability, links, and critical, yet important, differences between the genres. The presentation of disorienting relationships and properties may seem untamable at a glance, but through a keen eye and understanding of game mechanics and design, the similarities emerge quite proficiently. It is important to note that a consistent genre category does not exist due to the inconsistencies and evolution of genres, but there have been significant attempts at categorizing the video games through the playability, structure of the virtual world, and player's experience.

Chris Crawford was one of the original researchers of this phenomenon and in 1997 created a taxonomy of computer games. In 1997, even though there were consoles readily available to the public, computer games were a primary source of entertainment for video gamers and thus this taxonomy focuses upon the computer medium. However, many of these genres created and reported by Crawford could also have been applied to the console generation.

It is important to note that Crawford himself alleged "I do not claim that the taxonomy I propose is the correct one, nor will I accept the claim

that any correct taxonomy can be formulated" (pg. 25) actively acknowledging the profound nature of attempting to create a taxonomy which
would encompass every piece of detail pertaining to the idea of video game
genres.

Crawford's taxonomy consisted of two supergenres: *skill-and-action games*
(emphasizing perceptual and motor skills) and *strategy games* (emphasizing
cognitive effort). The reasoning for these specific classifications were that
skill-and-action games were "characterized by real-time play, heavy emphasis
on graphics and sound, and use of joysticks or paddles rather than a keyboard"
(pg. 26) and that *strategy games* "emphasized cogitation rather than manipulation" (pg. 30). A further delineation Crawford was clear to make was the
distinguishing factor between the two supergenres being that skill-and-action
games required a form of motor skills in order to be proficient and play while
strategy games (at least in this point of time before games such as StarCraft
and Warcraft) did not require the same or similar motor skills.

Within both supergenres were six individual *subtypes* or *subgenres*. For *skill-
and-action games* the six subtypes of subgenres were *combat games, maze games,
sports games, paddle games, race games*, and *miscellaneous games*. Within the
strategy games supergenre were six subgenres of *adventures, D&D games, war-
games, games of chance, educational and children's games*, and *interpersonal games*.

Table 3.1 Crawford's Taxonomy.

SUPERGENRES	
Skill & Action Games	*Strategy Games*
↓ *Subgenres*	↓
Combat Games	Adventures
Maze Games	Dungeons & Dragons Games
Sports Games	Wargames
Paddle Games	Games of Chance
Race Games	Educational and Children's Games

Adapted from Crawford (1997)

Since Crawford's taxonomy however, video game supergenres and
subgenres have evolved and increased significantly.

After Crawford's well received attempt at categorizing video games, Mark Wolf was a subsequent researcher to make a serious attempt at cataloging the even larger medium into categories in 2002. The primary difference in how each researcher categorized their taxonomies was Crawford focused on the skills needed for the individual to be successful within the gameplay of the video game and Wolf fostered a more critical idea focusing upon the player's experience within the interactivity components of the video game. While it still applied similar characteristics of Crawford's ideas, Wolf added the important component of player's subjective experience of the video game itself.

A major critique of Wolf's towards creating the genre list was that some of his conceived genres (e.g. Demo, Diagnostic, and Utility were given as primary examples) could arguably not be considered a game due to their inherent nature of programming. What he meant was that some video games have game-like elements, but do not comprise an entirety of what a game is. An example he gave of this was Mario Teaches Typing. In this computer game, Mario runs across the screen jumping to catch bricks and "stomp" turtles similar to his debut video game Mario Bros on the Nintendo Entertainment System (NES). The catch is the player has to type the letter correctly in order to continue forward. In essence, it is a program which teaches the player how to type and not used to entertain the senses—not a true video game.

Therefore, Wolf outlined his classification of video game genres based upon the developed categorization by the Library of Congress Moving Image Genre-Form Guide compiled originally by Brian Taves, Judi Hoffman, and Karen Lund (Wolf, 2002). His thinking of basing his taxonomy upon this classification was the rigorousness required to be accepted by the Library of Congress. He additionally cited other explanations by the description of the video game genres, articulation, and demarcation of distinctive and exhaustive typologies found within and between the relative genres.

In total, Wolf's finalized list consists of 42 different categories.

While the list may appear comprehensive, it was and still is not considered exhaustive and many of the categories had strong similarities at the time it was created. Since his taxonomy was produced much has changed even to the point that some of the genres he used do not exist any longer or have been melded into other categories.

Thomas Apperley, another games scholar, was additionally highly critical of the previously created video game genres because of the constant state of fluctuation and change declaring "they cannot be regarded as a consistent medium" (2006, pg. 6). Apperley asserted that arriving at the idea of clustering

Table 3.2 Wolf's Taxonomy

Abstract	Catching	Driving	Management Simulation	Puzzle	Sports
Adaption	Chase	Educational	Maze	Quiz	Strategy
Adventure	Collecting	Escape	Obstacle Course	Racing	Table-Top
Artificial Life	Combat	Fighting	Pencil & Paper	Role-Playing	Target
Board Games	Demo	Flying	Pinball	Rhythm & Dance	Text Adventure
Capturing	Diagnostic	Gambling	Platform	Shoot 'Em up	Training
Card Games	Dodging	Interactive Movie	Programming Games	Simulation	Utility

Adapted from Wolf (2002)

video games into genres from conclusions based upon video game aesthetic features, rather than the ergodic interactions taking place from the inside of the virtual world, was faulty. An ergodic interaction is how a video gamer or virtual player participates in a general action, set of interactions, or events within the virtual realm. This key point inspired a change of classifying video game genres, stemming primarily from the playability of and within the game rather than the superficial characteristics. This permitted a superior and more nuanced understanding of the video game itself in order to appropriately represent itself within a genre instead of a casual and causal glance which may have misconstrued non-similar video games as similar. Viewing a taxonomy from this point of reference, Apperley was able to correct his second critique of the classification of video games—that the larger issue for video game genres is their heavy emphasis upon "diverse representation strategies at the expense of other common features" (Apperley, 2006; Caldwell, 2004).

The key drawback of creating a taxonomy from this point of view is that the proposed genres are assessed from a heavily conservative approach producing a significantly reduced genre list. As a result, Apperley's list was significantly smaller than Wolf's and Crawford's, ending with four main differentiating genres: *simulation, strategy, action,* and *role-playing*.

A more recent taxonomy was proposed in 2013 by Steffan McAllister. McAllister created his taxonomy based upon the premise that genres are defined by the set of gameplay challenges found within the virtual world. In particular, the classification between genres exists based independently of the setting of the video game (i.e. land, seas, space, etc.), but constructed upon the gameplay—similar to Apperley's and Wolf's ideological pursuits to video game genres. Based upon those principles, McAllister's genres consisted of eleven genres overall: *action, action-adventure, adventure, horrors, racing, shoot em' ups, simulations, sport simulations, strategy, role-playing,* and *other*. This may be seen as a progression to a greater understanding of the nuances of video game genres, but McAllister additionally openly acknowledged the malleability of video game genres, and believed any subsequent video games created would be classified within his classification.

However, similarities exist between McAllister's proposed genres while other genres he noted can be subsumed under the other larger supergenres or consist of its own supergenre. An example of this would be the *horror* genre, in that it could be included as an *action-adventure* subgenre, or a *shoot em' up* could even be considered a subgenre of *action*. Furthermore, *role playing games* were incorporated into the *horror* genre when they should be considered a distinct category of itself. Due to these difficulties, McAllister's genres are reorganized to reflect a more appropriate supergenre list consisting of current video games and their subgenres. It is important to note that this proposed list may be considered non exhaustive and erroneous with time due to the constant flux of the video game genres. However, the genre list below will still be a viable source of information for individuals seeking an explanation of supergenres.

Video Game Genres

As video game genres are inconsistent and ever changing, it is important to keep the categorization of video game supergenres broad, but succinct in order to appropriately define them and the characteristics which make them individually unique. Therefore the list below is an attempt at a taxonomy using the previous researcher's ideological stances. Indeed, the playability, interactivity, and player's experiences are of importance when deciding discerning factors of a taxonomy of this magnitude. As a result, I put video games into seven discreet genres dependent upon the macro characteristics of the gameplay, the nuances of the worlds, and the experiences which can unfold through the player's experience: *action, adventure, action-adventure, role-playing, simulation, strategy,* and *other.* Through this interpretation, integration of the surrounding personality and play motivation research can also be explained within each genre providing a distinctive understanding of the video gamer who plays this type of the video game. However, an explanation of the genres is required in order to appropriately understand the latter.

Action

Action video games challenge the video gamer in tests of physical skill, high reaction speeds, and superior hand-eye coordination (Crawford, 1997). Additionally, the action genre incorporates other elements that are not considered to be central to game play such as races, puzzles, challenges, and exploration demands (Apperley, 2006; Crawford, 1997). Individuals playing action video games are usually under a time pressure to complete an objective while maintaining heightened attention and cognitive processes to meet the demands of the video game. *Shoot em' ups, platform, shooter, fighting,* and *stealth* video games can be considered subgenres of action because the video game player controls a majority of the action within the virtual realm, requiring a heightened use of the visual senses and increased reaction times (McAllister, 2013).

Usually found in these newer subgenres are ranged and melee weapons with differing, or a rotation of, heroes controlling the weapon while the player controls the movement, action, and weapon discharging of the hero. Video game players usually find themselves burdened with tactical and exploration challenges imposed upon them with a time limit creating an urgency to complete a mission or objective. The common goal of action games is to defeat the end of the game boss and the linear storyline of the game will bring the player to the objective automatically by defeating each level. However, multiplayer has become a larger focus of action games due to the ability of playing versus friends and incorporation of more people into the game. Examples of video games in this area are Doom, Quake, Overwatch, Super Mario Brothers, Double Dragon, Super Smash Brothers, Call of Duty, Counter Strike, Metal Gear, Hitman, Street Fighter, and Donkey Kong.

Adventure

Adventure video games originally began with computer text adventures where the player had to move the character with keyboard arrows and use written command prompts in order to progress through the game (Crawford, 1997; Wolf, 2002). These video games eventually evolved into more elaborate interfaces with controls and graphics as technology increased, expanding the controls of the player and interactivity of the gameplay. The player assumes a role as a protagonist within the video game storyline via the narrative driven gameplay. Reflex challenges or action within the game is usually not a focus or part of the game play, as action games require (Apperley, 2006). Most of the time the videogame's world is designed for one player, but on occasion some adventure video games do rely on team play. Through this type of gameplay, the player is thrust through a linear and plot-driven narrative with the singular focus of completing the adventure. Exploration of the virtual field is possible, however, there are multiple obstacles and barriers in place thwarting the player from entering different areas until they acquire a tool in order to scale the impediment. The blockades serve to drive the character and player in the singular and linear direction of the storyline utilizing objects found along the way (Wolf, 2002). Within the narrative of the video game there are puzzle rooms and challenges which require the player to think about the concepts within a room or environment in order to proceed in smaller steps which lead to a greater and grander prize. However, the player often has to backtrack to previous areas visited in order to unlock new items or information. Objectives may be unlocking doors and different rooms, retrieving objects, carrying objects, or using hand weapons to advance to the next room or area. A well written narrative and linear transitional state of storyline leads the player to become immersed and encounters within the virtual world to take on an important meaning for the player leading them to play many hours at a time while losing track of time.

Examples of video games in this genre are Haunted House, Myst, Professor Layton, The Walking Dead series, the original Metroid series, Heavy Rain, King's Quest, The Secret of Monkey Island, and The Longest Journey.

Action-Adventure

Action-adventure genre games consist of elements found in both action and adventure video games making them a hybrid of the two genres (Crawford, 1997; Wolf, 2002). *Action-adventure* springs into existence as *adventure* began to decline in popularity as a result of slower moving scenarios. It is a broad genre encompassing many different video games. Usually to progress in the game, the player is required to obtain a tool or in-game item used to overcome larger obstacles or enemies found within the virtual world, much like the *adventure* genre. Within the virtual world of *action-adventure*, there are consistent smaller obstacles which require navigation, combat, gathering, and simple to complex puzzle solving in order to progress. The story is enacted through the gameplay rather than narratively driven (Apperley, 2006; Wolf, 2002). Reflex skills are relied upon during parts of combat to dodge or advance on an enemy, although puzzles are more common than combat scenarios, requiring a constant cognitive process to think through the conniving riddles. The storyline is, again, linear and goal driving like the adventure genre with advanced mechanics such as an inventory system, numerous interactional events, and cut scenes with other non-playable characters. These games tend to focus heavily on exploration and item-gathering through open and closed world gameplay, essentially "leveling up" the played character. There usually is a clear delineation of enemy, hero, and populace, to be rescued or saved through the storyline and developed from the beginning of the video game.

Within this specific genre, there are many distinct subgenres, but many researchers and video gamers consider this genre to be in a constant state of flux because it is a broad category (Apperley, 2006). For instance, horror video games such as Dead Space fall into this classification mixing action, reflex, and adventure, but with an additional horror element, such as a zombie-like antagonist. Sandbox and Open World games like Minecraft are action-adventure even though the environment is consistently generating new and original content at any one time. Stealth games similar to Assassin's Creed fall into this category with an emphasis of avoiding detection while completing objectives, leading to a significant increase in world exploration to complete the game tasks. Other notable video game franchises which fall into this category are Resident Evil, Far Cry, Metroid Prime, Half Life, Portal, Dishonored, Tomb Raider, The Legend of Zelda, Banjo-Kazooie, Silent Hill, and Dishonored.

Role-Playing

Role-playing video games owe their ancestry to similar role-playing board games like Dungeons & Dragons and World of Warcraft. They are commonly referred to as Role Playing Games (RPGs) or Computer Role Playing Games

(CRPGs). The video game player specializes in a specific set of skills and role for group or solo adventuring (Crawford, 1997; Wolf, 2002). Immersion is exceptionally common in this genre due to the layout of the virtual world, well-defined character composition customization, storyline, and solo and group play. The storyline of the game can either be linear or non-linear with progression mandatory for continual character development. Players must venture through a large virtual overworld inhabited with monsters of varying character levels. In order to progress through this type of game, you must continue to advance to higher levels, acquiring experience points and obtaining stronger weapons and clothing referred to as "gear" (Wolf, 2002) Character development is usually the main focal point of the video game and fighting monsters in the virtual world is considered to be in "real-time" meaning instantaneous and continual instead of turn based where everyone has time to complete their turn before other individuals play again (McAllister, 2013). Most storylines portray and task the video game player with saving the world or society being threatened.

Story progression and development are key characteristics of this genre with numerous quests abound in the game allowing the player to complete the quest and obtain experience, gear, or reputation with an in-game faction. Players issue commands through their controller for their character which in turn performs them at an effectiveness determined numerically by the avatar's attributes, characteristics, gear, and level or skill (Wolf, 2002). While in most video games the story continues through level progression, in RPGs there are different choices for progression through the game such as joining a faction, guild, or killing a specific antagonist. On occasion, game elements may even be triggered just by traversing into a new "zone" or area of the video game. Exploration is a key component of RPGs, causing even deeper levels of immersion and the need to explore and see the different aspects the game can offer. Each zone usually has a specific and different feel to it allowing the player to experience a vast array of gameplay at their own pace. These games are usually exceptionally vast and time consuming in order to progress.

Video games which fall into this category are World of Warcraft, Diablo, Deus Ex, Baldur's Gate, Final Fantasy, Eve Online, EverQuest, Ultima Online, Runescape, the Mass Effect series, and Pokemon.

Simulation

Simulation is one of the most diverse categories of video games genres and attempts to replicate "real-life" in the form of virtual reality for entertainment, job training, prediction, or analysis of situational outcomes (Apperley, 2006; Wolf, 2002). Almost anything can be simulated for replicability within one of these games. Usually there are few, if any, goal oriented actions within these games besides experiencing different livable and life scenarios; however, there are simulation based games that attempt to test the creator, the video game player, of how much can be handled emotionally, spiritually, athletically, or even mechanically. Sports video games series like Madden and NBAK fall into this area also, imitating actual sports play in a virtual environment. As such, *racing* and *sports simulations* can be considered subgenres of this category (McAllister, 2013).

Other popular simulation video games are The Sims 1–4, pinball, Monster Rancher, SimFarm, SimCity, Black and White, Global Domination, FIFA, Rollercoaster Tycoon, the Need for Speed series, Truck Simulator, Goat Simulator, Flight Simulator, and the EA Sports series.

Strategy

Strategy video games have a greater focus on careful, methodical, and skillful, planning to win. In most *strategy* genre video games, the individual creates, manages, and controls units within the virtual world in order to achieve victory against a computer or another human adversary. To achieve faster or unique victories, many strategy games will allow exploitation of in-game scenarios such as economies, subjugation, and religion-based conditional victories (Wolf, 2002). A player must use all in-game mechanics to their advantage to plan a series of actions against opponents and defeat them using the game system bonuses to add to their chance of victory.

There are various strategy game subgenres such as real-time strategy (RTS), turn-based strategy (TBS), turn-based tactics (TBT), real-time tactics (RTT), multiplayer online battle arenas (MOBAs), and tower defense. Real-time video games do not progress in turns, but simultaneously as every player is continually creating, managing, and controlling units in an attempt to destroy the other avatars all at the same time (Apperley, 2006). In order to accomplish this, most strategy game players have "hotkeys" which allow them to greatly increase their ability to manage multiple base operations with the touch of a few buttons. Turn-based video games are exactly as they sound; distinct periods of turn-based actions which each play has time to assess their next move (Wolf, 2002). Each player gets one turn in which to input commands and then the control moves onto the next player in line, similar to a board game (McAllister, 2013). Multiplayer online battle arena games are where the player controls a single character on a team with other players who can be NPCs or actual video gamers. The primary objective is to destroy the other team's base, but generally there are barriers to accomplishing this such as minions, gates, towers, and even other players. Characters have varying abilities which grow in strength as the character levels up and can be enhanced through items collected. Tower defense games have a simple layout where computer controlled "creeps" move along a defined path and the video gamer has to put towers along the path in order to kill the creeps through damage, slowing down their speed, and even poisoning the creep.

An important distinction between strategy and tactics is how troops or combat is utilized in the game. Tactics refer to the utilization of troops in combat. An example of tactics would be to use characters who can handle large amounts of damage or have strong avoidance characteristics in the front of battle while weaker characters who would perish easier are in the back playing a more supportive role. Strategy describes the mixed usage of troops, combat bonuses, landscape where the battle ensues, and commander used in battle.

Common strategy games are Civilization, Master of Orion, Endless Space, Age of Empires, Starcraft, Warcraft, Command and Conquer, Risk, Clash of Clans, League of Legends, Defense of the Ancients, and Heroes of the Storm.

Other

The *other* video game category is reserved for video games which do not fit into a single category such as music, party, programming, puzzle, electronic board games, trivia, etc. This area is set aside for video games without a distinct genre yet may fit into multiple genres at once therefore requiring a new or more specific classification (McAllister, 2013).

Motivational Factors of Play

Player typologies and motivations have only recently been developed over the past decade. Scholars have provided their own quasi-lexicons to identify personality traits of individual behaviors during play in an attempt to classify gamer typology from Multi User Dungeons (MUD's) and other virtual world video games (Bartle, 2003, 2004; Fullerton, 2008; Radoff, 2011a, 2011b). A MUD is a real-time virtual world that is based entirely on text and was one of the first online virtual environments allowing people to interact with it (Bartle, 2003, 2004).

Table 3.3 Bartle's Player Types

Bartle's Player Types	Main Style of Play
Achievers	Play within the virtual world to attain and accomplish hard goals therefore giving an intrinsic sense of achievement through the progression.
Socializers	Interact with other players in the virtual world and find the greatest satisfaction of playing the video game from these interactions.
Explorers	Explore the virtual realms and find pleasure and excitement from discovering new areas and gaining knowledge of the newly discovered areas.
Killers	Find it enjoyable to dominate other players' within the virtual world by attacking, killing, or making other players general experience of the game hard or annoying.

Adapted from Bartle (2003).

Between 1989 and 1990 a lengthy debate broke out among users of MUD's online forums to answer Richard Bartle's, a professor of computer science and co-inventor of Multi User Dungeons (MUD's), question: "What do people want out of a MUD?" Bartle (2003, 2004) examined and identified four player categories from the investigation and centered on the in-game play styles of *Achiever, Socializer, Explorer,* and *Killers.*

Bartle later reformulated his model to include additional variations of the original four types after observing that players vacillated between the player typologies that he initially identified. In an attempt to adjust for these fluctuations, Bartle added another dimension to the traditional model (implicit and explicit variations of the original four types), establishing eight more player types—*Opportunists, Planners, Hackers, Scientists, Friends, Networkers, Griefers,* and *Politicians* (Bartle, 2004, 2005).

Bartle's Player types promoted the concept that players' engagement with their environments *within* the video game can be categorized by the specific preferences and choices of play (Bartle, 2004; 2005). This was one of the first attempts at viewing virtual worlds from the video game player's perspective and play demands, rather than pure observable factors.

Since the originally taxonomy of MMOs, Bartle's model has been criticized and reiterated upon due to the exclusions of motivations of play for the video gamer and their genre of focus (Fullerton, 2008; Radoff, 2011a, 2011b; Yee, 2006). Radoff (2011a) rebuked the categorization of Bartle's player's typology due to overemphasizing some concepts over others, a lack of concreteness

Table 3.4 Bartle's Revised Typology

Bartle's Player Types	Implicit/Explicit	Style of Play
Achievers	Opportunists (Implicit)	Try to take advantage of any given situation and tend to avoid challenges.
	Planners (Explicit)	More calculating with their actions—attributing everything to a larger scheme/plan.
Socializers	Friends (Implicit)	Mainly interact with people they have already established relationships with.
	Networkers (Explicit)	Seek out people to interact with based on assessing and getting to know them.
Explorers	Hackers (Implicit)	Experiment to reveal meaning and seek to discover new phenomena.
	Scientists (Explicit)	Experiment to form theories and explain new phenomena.
Killers	Griefers (Implicit)	Very much in the player's personal space with the aim to obtain a menacing and annoying reputation.
	Politicians (Explicit)	Manipulate people accordingly to suit their needs as well as act with well-developed foresight to accomplish their goals.

Adapted from Bartle (2005).

in the typology, and over-broad categorization of play styles. Radoff (2011a) further criticized Bartle's model by suggesting that it rejected various and important video game player motivations. However, Bartle himself has taken a stance against this criticism, stating that his taxonomy should not be used outside of the original intention of MUDs otherwise it may not be appropriately extrapolated and understood (Bartle, 2012).

Regardless, from these criticisms, Radoff approached the concept of player typologies to account for user types in a more succinct way. Radoff proposed a revised approach that aimed to cater to all user types with four alternative categorizations based upon observable goals of social interaction and the notion that video game players will evolve in their play styles over time (Radoff, 2011a).

Table 3.5 Radoff's Player Types

Radoff's Player Types	Main Style of Play
Immersion	Stories, role playing, exploration, imagination, and a sense of connectedness to the world of the game.
Achievement	Sense of progress, mastery of skills and knowledge, etc.
Cooperation	Player involvement in activities, helping each other, through creativity, shared adversity, etc.
Competition	Player involvement where individuals compete over scarce resources, comparison, and win/loss situations.

Adapted from Radoff (2011a)

Table 3.6 Fullerton's Player Types

Fullerton's Player Types	Style of Play
The Competitor	Plays to best other players, regardless of the game.
The Explorer	Curious about the world, loves to adventure; seeks outside boundaries, physical or mental.
The Collector	Acquires items, trophies, or knowledge; likes to create sets, organize history, etc.
The Achiever	Plays for varying levels of achievement; ladders and levels incentivize the achiever.
The Joker	Doesn't take the game seriously—plays for the fun of playing; there's a potential for jokers to annoy serious players, but on the other hand, jokers can make the game more social than competitive.
The Artist	Driven by creativity, creation, design.
The Director	Loves to be in charge, direct the playing.
The Storyteller	Loves to create or live in worlds of fantasy and imagination.
The Performer	Loves to put on a show for others.
The Craftsman	Wants to build, craft, engineer, or puzzle things out.

Adapted from Fullerton (2008)

While Radoff (2011a) focused on broader categories he believed encompassed all video gamers, Tracy Fullerton (2008) outlined ten different types of players based upon personal agendas, play, and individual needs found inside virtual realities. She included the video gamer's point of view and choices when creating her taxonomy of play styles.

Finally, Nick Yee (2006) researched Bartle's model through a large study of 3,000 MMORPG players and utilized factor analysis reducing player motivations to the three distinct areas of Achievement, Social, and Immersion with subcategories of each. Through the analysis, Yee suggested the subcategories did not have enough theoretical and statistical basis to be considered full player types.

Yee finished with his conceptualization of video gamer motivations. With the help of Nicolas Ducheneaut, they created a company called "Quantic Foundry" primarily aimed at identifying video game motivation profiles. They established psychometric methods and data from over 220,000 video

Table 3.7 Yee's Player Types

Yee's Player Types	Subcategory	Motivation
Achievement	Advancement	Progress, power, accumulation, status.
	Mechanics	Numbers, optimization, templating, analysis.
	Competition	Challenging others, provocation, domination.
Social	Socializing	Casual chat, helping others, making friends.
	Relationship	Personal, self-disclosure, find and give support.
	Teamwork	Collaboration, groups, group achievements.
Immersion	Discovery	Exploration, lore, finding hidden things.
	Role-Playing	Story line, character history, roles, fantasy.
	Customization	Appearances, accessories, style, color schemes.
	Escapism	Relax, escape from real life, and avoid real life problems.

Adapted from Yee (2006)

gamers to develop an empirical model of video gamer motivations called the "Gamer Motivational Model" (Yee & Ducheneaut, 2017).

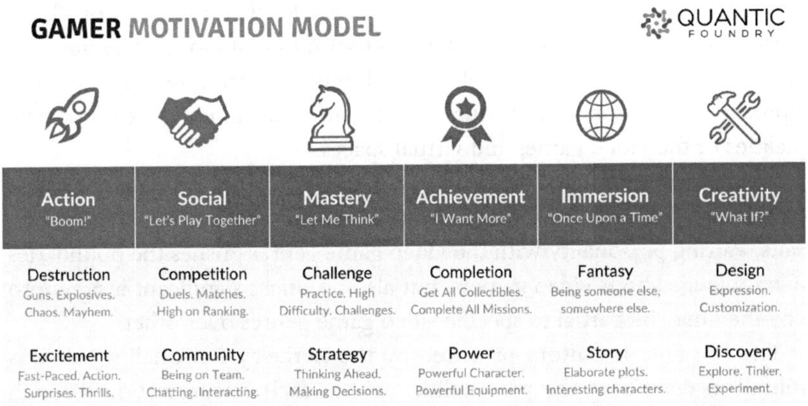

Action	Social	Mastery	Achievement	Immersion	Creativity
"Boom!"	"Let's Play Together"	"Let Me Think"	"I Want More"	"Once Upon a Time"	"What If?"
Destruction	**Competition**	**Challenge**	**Completion**	**Fantasy**	**Design**
Guns. Explosives. Chaos. Mayhem.	Duels. Matches. High on Ranking.	Practice. High Difficulty. Challenges.	Get All Collectibles. Complete All Missions.	Being someone else, somewhere else.	Expression. Customization.
Excitement	**Community**	**Strategy**	**Power**	**Story**	**Discovery**
Fast-Paced. Action. Surprises. Thrills.	Being on Team. Chatting. Interacting.	Thinking Ahead. Making Decisions.	Powerful Character. Powerful Equipment.	Elaborate plots. Interesting characters.	Explore. Tinker. Experiment.

Figure 3.1 Gamer Motivational Model

Artwork by Yee & Ducheneaut (2017), Used with permission

Overall, they found twelve motivation factors which video gamers use to choose and play a video game. They then used hierarchical clustering to detect groupings of the twelve motivations and determine which ones were similar, resulting in six overarching frameworks of motivations. What is most interesting about these results is they show how motivations of play are *related to one another*, a first for this area of research. This is important because it suggests that play and motivation are important factors of game choice because of the experience sought and found in specific genres, motivations, and players. Overall, each taxonomy has important aspects of play and there are certainly many similarities between them, but the most important aspect identified is that video gamers use and play video games for different reasons, suggesting a multitude of explorations to be acknowledged therapeutically.

Personality Profiles within the Genres

As clinicians and experts, we observe personality and the traits, or smaller parts of personality, by watching and listening to people and their patterns of behaviors and thoughts. Personality and behavior must be viewed through a multitude of interactions in order to be seen clearly. Observing different play structures within video games is no different. Different behaviors and character play define how the individual is playing, but also define *how the individual interacts with others* including the in-game Non-Playable Characters (NPCs). At times it may be considered griefing (causing grief to another player, kill stealing, or killing them when they are a lower level and flagged for Player versus Player interactions) while during other moments socially helping out another player. Just like in real life, different scenarios require different approaches. This important feature is critical in understanding the immersive qualities of the video games and virtual spaces.

Personality is a crucial factor in understanding an individual on a much more in-depth and expansive manner through observable intrinsic and extrinsic traits. Pairing personality with the video game genres pushes the boundaries of knowledge about video gamers, but also produces significant insight into why they may be partial to specific video game genres over others.

The Big Five Inventory procured by the Berkeley Personality Lab was utilized in describing the personalities within each categorization through one of the largest studies performed on video gamers and personality. The study resulted in 19,416 video gamers participating. The Big Five Inventory consists of measuring five differentiating personality characteristics: **openness to experience** (*inventive/curious* vs. *consistent/cautious*), **conscientiousness** (*efficient/organized* vs. *easy-going/careless*), **extraversion** (*outgoing/energetic* vs. *solitary/reserved*), **agreeableness** (*friendly/compassionate* vs. *cold/unkind*), and **neuroticism** (*sensitive/nervous* vs. *secure/confident*) (Atkinson, Atkinson, Smith, Bem, & Nolen-Hoeksema, 2000; Bean, 2015; John, Donahue, & Kentle, 1991; John, Naumann, & Soto, 2008).

Latent Profile Analysis, the statistical analysis method used, focused on classifying individuals into homogenous categories representing classes of subgroups within each genre. Through the examination of observed responses on the BFI it evaluated the responses and created a pattern based upon how many individuals responded similarly. Four general personality profiles emerged from within the seven video game supergenres; each with different variations.

The discovered profiles had statistically different scores on the BFI when compared to each other, signifying differentiating personalities gravitating towards preferred genres. The four personality profiles were named Introversive, Extroversive, Secure Ambiversive, and Insecure Ambiversive because of the qualities exhibited on the Big Five Inventory traits (Bean, 2015; Cohen & Schmidt, 1979; Eysenck; 1971; Goldberg, 1992; Ryckman, 2004). Introversive video game players had higher neuroticism, but lower scores in the other four BFI domains, Extroversive players had lower neuroticism scores, but higher scores in the four areas, while the Ambiversive classes' scores fell in the middle of Introversive and Extroversive, but differed on the neuroticism

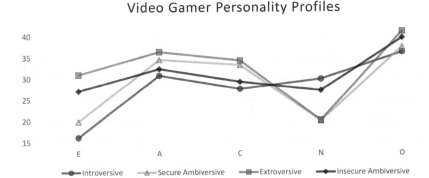

Figure 3.2 Video Gamer Personality Profiles

scores independently (Bean, 2015). The Secure Ambiversive's lower levels of neuroticism suggests an ability to handle emotionally charged gameplay whereas the Insecure Ambiversive's profile had higher levels of neuroticism and may not be able to adjust as easily or readily.

Evaluating which video gamer personalities gravitated towards specific video game genres resulted in interesting findings. Overall, all four personality profiles were found across the seven video game genres varying in use.

Examining which profiles were found in each of the different genres of video gaming provides more insight into which types of video gamers gravitate towards specific genres. The action genre primarily had Secure Ambiversive profiles with Insecure Ambiversive profiles closely following in numbers. This may be because of the pressure to complete a task in a specific amount of given time which Ambiversive individuals may have an easier time completing. The adventure genre similarly reported Insecure and Secure Ambiversive profiles suggesting puzzle and non-confrontational game play may be of importance to these personality profiles. The action/adventure genre had Introversive, Secure Ambiversive, and Insecure Ambiversive profiles. The Introversive personality profile was found primarily suggesting introversive video game players gravitate towards this type of genre quite possibly due to the individualistic mechanics and low interactions with other people. The role-playing genre was the only genre to have all four personality profiles emerge suggesting that the role-playing genre has characteristics and meets needs of all four personality profiles, therefore making it a versatile gaming world. The last three genres, simulation, strategy, and other, each only had Introversive and Extroversive profiles found suggesting these personality types dominate these genres.

Table 3.8 Video Gamer Personality Profiles

Genre	Introversion	Extroversion	Secure Ambiversive	Insecure Ambiversive
Action	–	–	X	X
Adventure	–	–	X	X
Action/Adventure	X	–	X	X
Role-playing	X	X	X	X
Simulation	X	X	–	–
Strategy	X	X	–	–
Other	X	X	–	–

The idea of introversion and extraversion was first proposed as a central dimension of personality by Carl Jung (1921). This is typically viewed as a single continuum of human personality. For example, being high in one element such as extroversion means the individual is lower in the other trait of introversion dependent upon the context of the situation for the individual. The findings of four personality profiles appearing in the sample of video gamers gives credence to Jung's ideas that the continuum is inherent in every individual and that while one typology may play a larger role, both can be present (Eysenck, 1971; Ryckman, 2004). Introversive personalities focus on their inner psychic reality as a way of understanding the world; whereas in contrast, extroversive personalities primarily look outwards to their social environment for their grounding in life. Introversive personalities are thought to become overwhelmed and drained of their energy while connecting in face to face interactions socially, while in contrast the extroversive is revitalized (Eysenck, 1971; Jung, 1921). Extroversive personalities tend to enjoy spending most of their time in social environments and their sense of self is based on their external interactions. They can also become bored when they are in more solitary environments because of the lack of social engagement (Jung, 1921; Ryckman, 2004). Ambiversive personalities have traits and attributes of both Extroversive and Introversive personalities dependent upon their needs at the time (Cohen & Schmidt, 1979). Although it is important to note that the BFI's ideas of extroversion are not conceptually based upon Jung's ideology and may differ through current psychological usage.

However, they can be considered to be similar as Jung's definition focused on an individual's orientation to psychic contents (i.e. looking to the outside world or within the individual for meaning in one's life) and the BFI is marked by an individual's interaction and engagement with the outside world (i.e. extraversion for high interaction and introversion for low engagement). In both situations, the individual is interacting with their internal psychic mechanisms either within themselves or from the external world in attempts to make meaning and understanding of their lives (Jung, 1921; McCrae & Costa, 1991).

Ambiversive personality video gamers, theoretically, are moderately comfortable with groups, social interaction, being in unknown places, and generally out and about similar to extroversive video gamers. The important other side of an Ambiversive personality is the person additionally enjoys and needs time away from everyone in order to recharge similar to the Introversive personality. As such, video gaming may provide the aforementioned security of still fulfilling their extroversive side, but at a safe distance through a video game in order not to overpower their intrapsychic processes and rejuvenation creating anxiety.

Introversive personalities may utilize video games as a method of enjoyment in interacting with social environments without becoming overwhelmed or drained and/or an appropriate or safe method of interpersonal interaction for Introversive personalities. Therefore, video gaming may be considered a positive social interaction for many introversive personalities contrary to the societal belief (Hilgard, Engelhardt, & Bartholow, 2013) that video gamers are socially isolative and socially engaged individuals may not play video games. However, the Extroversive profile's presence in speculation, suggests some extroverts may still obtain personal satisfaction from virtual worlds, counter to public belief. Clearly there is more to know about video gamer's motivational principles and culture outside of the scope of common stereotypes.

Fullerton, Radoff, and Yee & Ducheneaut's (2008; 2011a, 2011b; 2006; 2017) revised typologies recognized the diversity of gamers and their motivations when it comes to engaging and interacting with virtual worlds while Bean's (2015) personality findings suggest many different personalities play video games and are drawn towards specific genres. In the case of such diversity with not only players, but also games, it is important to consider that more personal information is required in forming a more solid conceptualization of video game players societally and in our therapy offices. This information assists in distinguishing individual preferences to comprehensively identify what it is exactly that gamers are drawn to in virtual worlds.

Unfortunately, current beliefs of identifying and understanding video gamers do not take these important characteristics into consideration when viewing the video game in clinical therapeutic context. However, with careful consideration and an interest in the virtual world being played in, much more important information can be learned and utilized proficiently to further understand the video gamer seated in front of the therapist.

References

Apperley, T. H. (2006). Genre and game studies: Towards a critical approach to video game genres. *Simulation & Gaming, 37*(1), 6–23.

Atkinson, R. L.; Atkinson, R. C., Smith, E. E., Bem, D.J., & Nolen-Hoeksema, S. (2000). *Hilgard's Introduction to Psychology* (13 ed.). Orlando, FL: Harcourt College Publishers.

Bartle, R. A. (2003). Hearts, clubs, diamonds, spades: players who suit MUDs. In K. Salen & E. Zimmerman, (Eds). *The game design reader: A rules of play anthology* (p. 754–787). Cambridge, MA: MIT Press.

Bartle, R. A. (2004). *Designing virtual worlds*. Berkeley, CA: New Riders.

Bartle, R. A. (2005). Virtual worlds: Why people play. *Massively Multiplayer Game Development, 2*, 3–18.

Bartle, R. A. (2012). Player type theory: Uses and abuses. Retrieved from www.youtube.com/watch?v=ZIzLbE-93nc&feature=youtu.be.

Bean, A. (2015). Video gamers' personas: A five factor study exploring personality elements of the video gamer. Retrieved from ProQuest Digital Dissertations. (AAT 3726481).

Caldwell, N. (2004). Theoretical frameworks for analysing turn-based computer strategy games. *Media International Australia, 110*, 42–51.

Cohen, D., & Schmidt, J. P. (1979). Ambiversion: Characteristics of Midrange Responders on the Introversion-Extraversion Continuum. *Journal of Personality Assessment, 43*(5), 514–516.

Crawford, C. (1997). *The art of computer game design*. Vancouver, WA: Washington State University Vancouver.

Eysenck, H. J. (1971). *Readings in Extraversion–Introversion*. New York: Wiley.

Fullerton, T. (2008). *Game design workshop: A playcentric approach to creating innovative games*. Boston, MA: Morgan Kaufmann.

Goldberg, L. R. (1992). The development of markers for the Big-Five factor structure. *Psychological Assessment, 4*, 26–42.

Hilgard, J., Engelhardt, C. R., & Bartholow, B. D. (2013). Individual differences in motives, preferences, and pathology in videogames: The gaming attitudes, motives, and experiences scales (GAMES). *Frontiers In Psychology, 4*, 1–13.

John, O. P., Donahue, E. M., & Kentle, R. L. (1991). *The Big Five Inventory—Versions 4a and 54*. Berkeley, CA: University of California, Berkeley, Institute of Personality and Social Research.

John, O. P., Naumann, L. P., & Soto, C. J. (2008). Paradigm shift to the integrative big-five trait taxonomy: History, measurement, and conceptual issues. In O. P. John, R. W. Robins, & L. A. Pervin (Eds.), *Handbook of personality: Theory and research* (pp. 114–158). New York, NY: Guilford Press.

King. (2016). Farm Heroes Saga.

McAllister, S. (2013). *Video game genres*. Ebook: OxBo Publishing.

McCrae, R. R. & Costa, P. T. (1991). Adding liebe und arbeit: The full five-factor model and well-being. *Personality and Social Psychology Bulletin, 17*(2): 227–232.

Radoff, J. (2011a). *Game on: Energize your business with social media games*. Indianapolis, IN: Wiley Publishing, Inc.

Radoff, J. (2011b, May 19). Game player motivations. Retrieved from http://radoff.com/blog/2011/05/19/game-player-motivations/.

Ryckman, R. (2004). *Theories of personality*. Belmont, CA: Thomson/Wadsworth.

Supercell. (2012). Clash of Clans.

Yee, N. (2006). Motivations of play in online games. *Journal of CyberPsychology and Behavior, 9*, 772–775. doi:10.1089/cpb.2006.9.772.

Yee, N., & Ducheneaut, N. (2017). Gamer motivation model. Retrieved from https://quanticfoundry.com/#motivation-model.

Wolf, M. J. P. (2002). *The medium of the video game*. Austin, TX: University of Texas Press.

Video Games, Relationships, and Online Interpersonal Communication

4

Gary: Hey we need a new healer tonight, but your HPS need to be up there, I think you are geared, right?

Andrea: Definitely! I believe my HPS should be OK to deal with the DPS from the boss, what dungeon are you running?

Gary: Not a dungeon, but a raid. We start at 6PM our time and attempt multiple times until 10PM. What are your HPS anyways?

Andrea: Oh, I don't know if I am ready for that level yet, I just finished heroics and becoming attuned for the raids. My HPS is around 170 thousand.

Gary: Hmmm, that may be a little low, but your character spec is good for raid healing so I am sure we can make it work.

Andrea: Do you think I can mitigate the DPS enough? My spells hit hard, but also are not ticking as quickly as they should.

Gary: Only one way to find out! We will send you an invite tonight around raid time. Be ready.

Andrea: Sounds good, I will be ready for it and update my addons to make sure they can handle it.

Does this sound like communication to you? It should. This is a normal conversation between two video gamers who are planning to run a dungeon requiring more than the average amount of players, commonly called a raid. A raid usually requires more than a standard one to five players, and up to forty people. The topics talked about above pertain to the need for each player to pull their own weight in the group during a boss battle. If you were able to follow along, chances are you play video games and can understand the terminology easily enough. If not, then this chapter will bring you clarity and help you make sense of it all.

This chapter focuses on the intersections of Psychology and Communication Studies. While some scholars may argue the two areas of academia do not have enough commonalities, I disagree. Psychology, to briefly put it, is the study of the mind, motivations, intrinsic and extrinsic personality patterns, community, behaviors, and interpersonal relationships. Communication studies are more primarily focused on discourse analysis or a number of approaches to analyzing language, communication modes, and how we interact across different mediums including technology. While they do have substantial differences, online relationships and communication studies have more fellowship than differences. This chapter will not break the two apart, but speak about them as if they were one beginning with basic communication.

Communication

According to Weiten, Dunn, and Hammer, communication is "an interactional process in which one person sends a message to another" (2015, pg. 231). This means it involves at least two people and requires an action between the people. Communication may be verbal or nonverbal. Verbal communications are the words coming out of our mouths, the sentences, phrases, and other orally based or spoken sounds. Nonverbal communications are the gestures we use when talking to one another. The gestures can be hand motions (i.e. sign language), sitting with our legs crossed, hands tucked in our pockets, low eye contact, a smirk or smile on our face, our posture, how we walk, or varying postural looks we give to different stimuli. The important aspect is that there is no verbal or spoken communication; hence the name nonverbal.

One other important communiqué process piece in communication is bi-directional, or has a two-way meaning and is being sent both ways from one individual to another at any time. This may look, to an observer, like an individual who is verbally talking to someone and the person being talked to is nonverbally giving cues about what they are thinking through the posture being held, low eye contact, and looking around the immediate space appearing to be bored with the conversation.

Even though only one person is talking, another is sending a signal back to the person nonverbally constituting a two-way communicative meaning. For another example, an individual is raising their voice while talking to another person while the second individual has their arms crossed in front of them. This signifies the second person is not interested or closed to the communication being presented by the first person; in this example, most likely due to the raised voice. The communication process can be broken down even further into five components. They are:

1. The *sender* or person who begins the communication.
2. The *receiver* or the person the message is being presented to.
3. The *message* itself or the information being offered by the first person to the second individual.
4. The *channel* of the message or how the message reaches the receiver from the sender.
5. The *context* or environment where the communication takes place.

Each time a form of communication occurs, it can be easily placed into these constituents by reviewing the communication more carefully.

There are additional variables which require consideration dependent upon the communication context: type of language used, willingness of receiver to hear the message, noise or stimulus that interferes with expression or understanding the message, and tone in which the message is communicated. Without considering these additional variables, communication becomes distorted and misinterpreted. Much of the time, these variables are assumed to be inherent within the communicative apparatus and not thoughtfully engaged ultimately-interfering with the communication process.

Table 4.1 Distorted Communication Variables

Additional Variable	Example	Result
Language Used	Choice of words, different language spoken	Distorted Communication
Willingness to Hear	Is the receiver not willing to listen to the message?	
Noise	Anything causing the receiver to misinterpret the message: poor hearing, distractions, mispronunciation.	
Message Tone	Different Tones: angry, sad, disappointing, etc.	

Further important points to note are specific factors can complicate and distort communication between a sender and receiver: different beliefs, values, and the latitudes of acceptance and rejection. These influence the way the message is being sent and received, perceived, reacting to message, how the message is being understood, and whether the message is being accepted or rejected by the receiver. An example includes poor grammar and word choice while communicating; however, the message may still be understood if the receiver has the ability to see past this barrier and has a more diverse communication style. The larger difficulty in communication is whether the message is within the latitude of rejection, acceptance, or non-commitment for the receiver.

Sherif's (1963; see also Griffin, 2011) research on social judgment theory has illustrated three latitudes of personal opinion that everyone consistently holds for their own personal self and the acceptance or opposition of another's viewpoint. Sherif believed our attitudes consisted of three zones: the latitude of **acceptance, rejection**, and **non-commitment**. Our **acceptance** zone is the smallest because it is closest to our self and comprised of our core beliefs. It is followed by our **non-commitment** which is larger than the **acceptance** zone, but still smaller than the **rejection** portion because we tend to reject more ideas and opinions than accept them. Putting these three zones together results in the full spectrum of an individual's attitude (Sherif, 1963; Sherif, Sherif, & Nebergall, 1965).

Latitude	Attitude Zone
Acceptance	Ideas a person sees as similar to theirs
Non-commitment	Ideas that you feel indifferent towards
Rejection	Ideas a person sees as unreasonable

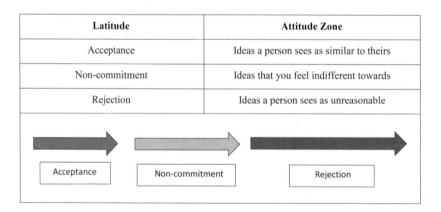

Figure 4.1 The Latitudes of Acceptance, Non-Commitment, and Rejection

In order to appropriately have the person be receptive to the message, the context of the message needs to align with the acceptance range or be persuasive enough within the non-commitment range, otherwise the message is lost. A message being lost is fairly common when discussing topics which are unfamiliar to the receiver, or in the case of this book, society and video game communication. Without being appropriately educated by scholars and practitioners, moral panic can easily take over and society looks for a scapegoat instead of using their critical thought. We will discuss this further in chapter five.

Computer Mediated Communication

Up to this point in this chapter, communication has been presented as an interaction between two or more individuals in the context of *face-to-face* communication; however, humans participate in other communicative manners and modes (Wright & Webb, 2011). This makes communication *multi-modal* or having the ability for multiple communication methods or mannerisms. The other communication area continuously growing in today's society is *computer-mediated-communication* (Jones, 1998; Wright & Webb, 2011). This communicative area consists through computers, smartphones, headphones, or any electronic device. This includes emails, texting, Facebook messaging, Skyping, and other computer or electronically mediated communication forms found in today's society.

Amidst these computer mediated communication mediums lay a different and unique society called "Geek Culture." It consists of more than just the video games that this book primarily focuses upon, and includes things such as Tumblr, Twitter, costume play (Cos-Play), card games (i.e. Magic the Gathering), retro-gaming, live action role playing (LARPing), Twitch, and Steam to name only a small portion. While this book gives great detail to the realm of video games, it does not provide an avenue in which to view "Geek Culture" in entirety.

Computer-mediated-communication is a hot and contentious debate currently due to polarized views of hype and hysteria also known as moral panic, which will be further expanded in Chapter 5. Polarized views are extreme theoretical assessments on a topic, technology, idea, or anything considered to be new or currently trending in society; in this case computer mediated relationships (Castells, 1996; Ess & Sudweeks, 2001). New information, progress, or societal change in fact, breeds the polarization of positive and negative views as Thurlow, Tomic, and Lengel suggest because there is "an associated period of social and cultural reorganization and reflection —and sometimes even anxiety and conflict" (2004, pg. 39). During this acclimation process, the two polarized camps are continuously viewing the new existent form, in this case video games, as extremely helpful or foreseeable or as detrimental to society, also known as technological determinism. In essence, technological determinism is a reductionist theory, meaning reducing to the smallest variable or explanation, which assumes society, societal structure, and cultural values are solely driven by technology. While technology may play a role in this area, it may be presumptuous to state it is the sole driving force. Technological determinism is not this chapter's supreme focus and therefore not discussed in more depth past this basic conceptualization. (See Thulow, Tomic and Lengel, 2014 for more information on technological determinism).

With computer-mediated-communication and communication via video games or online mediums, two allegations have been prominent in research and society. These assertions are that playing online video games are asocial or a form of negative communication and antisocial while having a negative impact on relationships outside the computer-mediated-communication or video game, and therefore detrimental to the gamer's communication abilities. The accusations are based on the distinct differences between face-to face and computer-mediated communications and primarily inserts the idea that the computers and technology are "noise" which distract and do not allow for appropriate communication to occur.

The main differences between face-to-face and computer-mediated communications are usually divided into five domains; physical distance, anonymity, communication richness, visual cues, and time. *Physical distance* in face-to-face communication is when at least two individuals have to meet at the same place and time in order to communicate whereas computer-mediated-communication is a medium in which people can meet and interact online at a great distance of thousands of miles away and across continents.

Communicative Deficits: Do They Exist?

Research has shown individuals communicating online take greater risks with their personal information than in face-to-face communications due to an *anonymity* factor and purports communication deteriorates or is not as *"rich"* through online communication methods (Thurlow, Tomic, & Lengel, 2004). Thurlow, Tomic, & Lengel (2004) claim this because individuals communicating through virtual means cannot see the visual cues or nonverbal communication another gives off as in face-to-face communication in real-time and therefore may be misconstrued as intending to mean something else than previous planned. We all have had this happen to us in some form as misreading the intent of an email or text message and taking it out of *context*. Contextual cues are much more difficult to interpret through computer-mediated communicative forms because there is a loss of direct face-to-face interaction with related verbal and nonverbal cues.

By misplacing the context of the communication, there are detrimental effects upon the individual reading or hearing the message propelled by the sender within the communication. However, with a different computer-mediated communication conceptualization providing different frameworks, this changes substantially. The previous accusations, that online communications and relationships are considered to be *deficit models* because hypothetically, a part of the communication structure is lost, changes. Lost is too strong: a better word describing what is actually occurring is "changed" and is a healthier defining word to discuss the entire concept. The communication itself hasn't been lost, it has just been altered in its contextual format.

Let us take Facebook as an example of computer-mediated communication. Facebook is comprised of an informational page about a person. Facebook lists an individual's history, details and updates about the individual, employment, hobbies, etc.; however, does it constitute the person in their entirety? Of course not. Facebook merely lists *facts* about them, not who they are, what personality they have, or what type of person they are. People who claim that Facebook can provide these things are confused with *their interpretation* of the *facts* listed upon the page and have become lost to the noise of the message. Researchers have focused upon these specificities of discussing the loss of communication: the distraction from the noise. Yes, to a point, you can profile someone's account and make general assumptions from the content, but not enough to definitively and accurately define the person.

This is where many youths misinterpret others online personas and *make assumptions* about other people's pages which in turn leads to bullying based on a psychological *projection and assumption* comprising the idea that the person's identity is created by the online profile. Bullying among youth has been and continues to be a difficult problem to solve, not just because of the anonymity factor through online interactions, but because youth and adolescence is a difficult time in everyone's life. Identity is forming in youth and the ego, or personal consciousness, is easily hurt or destroyed by careless comments. These events occur because the ego and self-concept has not yet differentiated. This progression happens later on in early adulthood rather than at the youth stage of development. We should not expect children and youths to have completed this differentiation when some adults never do.

Time is what is needed along with life experience in order to begin and eventually complete the process of individuation. While it is also important to recognize we should not have online bullying, it is likely to continue existing regardless of interventions placed upon it because society is becoming more technology bound. This further begs the question: Should we be more focused on helping our children build resilience to bullying instead of targeting the concept of bullying itself?

While communication has changed, using this Facebook analogy shows that it has not been lost. We still have the sender, receiver, message, channel, and context (see chart below). This is akin to a form of bullying which was prominent before the internet when individuals were being bullied in the streets or outside of the school for how they look. Individuals were picked on based on their looks and masculine/feminine attributes, not upon their inner selves. Again, it is about the person's shell or persona, not what lies inside or their psychological makeup. Development of the internal self may help to further eradicate bullying so noticeable in our world today.

Sender	Receiver	Message	Channel	Context
Bully →	Bullied →	Bullying →	Facebook →	About Page

Figure 4.2 Facebook Bullying Communication

The reader reading this book is another example of what constitutes communication. There are the words being read, the individual reading the words, the message attempting to be transcribed through the use of words, the book is the communication channel, and the book context is video games and social communication through different mediums. Overall, the communication is still present, just the context of the information and presentation changed.

Sender	Receiver	Message	Channel	Context
Words →	Reader →	Written Words →	Book →	Content of Book

Figure 4.3 Book Reading Communication

The premise of laying these foundational ideas found within the previous paragraphs was to prepare you, as the reader, for the following passages on video games, communication, and interpersonal relationships.

Video Game Communication

Generally video gamers are stereotyped as having no friends, no social or life skills, are obese, live in their parent's basement, and are inept at any form of relationship or communication. Fortunately, research on the matter has debunked these myths and stereotypes: investigations show many video gamers are fit and healthy, live independently, have intact social relationships, and thriving love lives. In fact, video game companies are now discussing the growing body of evidence that their games brought together love in many forms and created families. The research goes a step further suggesting video games and online behaviors are an important place for those who are insecurely attached to the outside world to experience expression, enjoyment, and interaction. In other words, individuals who experience anxiety from social communication, communication in general, low self-esteem, low self-confidence, and other anxious symptoms see online and video game interactions as a safe haven in which to connect and experience relationships and communications with others. Even though this may be viewed as a safe mechanism to interact with others, society views it as detrimental; therefore, because it does not fit into "normal methods" of communication, society places an unconscious negativity on video gamers, creating a negative perspective of the non-virtual world for the gamers. Anything in the history of the human race that has been considered "different" is ultimately labeled "bad" by our society. This results from lack of understanding the current phenomenon, but quickly dissipates once more knowledge is presented and the phenomenon is accepted as a "normal" part of society.

An example describing one of the most reported concerns video gamer parents and non-video game advocates alike have is the "lack of social interaction" when their child is playing video games. From a specific point of view, mainly not understanding what the video game can offer or considering at it from an outsider's vision, this can be presumed to be correct. Conversely, if one were to step inside the video game realm and look at the interaction types, one would see that it meets all the criteria for communication and healthy relationships.

While in play, the video gamer is interacting with others either over an additional program, such as Skype, Ventrilo or Discord sending and receiving messages through a medium or channel Electronic Device (E-Device), and/or portraying their avatar through emotes. There is a second additional step to provide the communication, but it continues to result in communication.

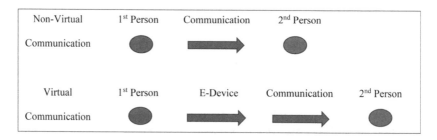

Figure 4.4 Virtual Versus Non-Virtual Communication

Emotes are a nonverbal method of communicating with other individuals playing the game. This form of communication describes an action and gesture which your avatar completes within the virtual realm. This indicates the player is communicating an action through the nonverbal communication, but not directly saying or using words. The message is usually contextualized about the game and a request for help, strategy, or role-playing. These meet all the requirements for communication, they are just completed using online equipment within a virtual realm. Again, communication exists, it has just been transformed into a new form or method, but meets all the criteria for basic communication.

Social Cues and Video Gamer Interpersonal Relationships

Some scholars discuss *social cue* deficits while interacting through video games. In video games or virtual worlds, social cues are not mandated in the same or similar manner as in the real world. In the real world, we need to sometimes see visual cues in order to create appropriate inferences. In virtual realms, there is usually a linear goal with a basic requirement of in-game social cues for participation. Through the learning of the in-game environment, leveling, and coaching from other players, social cues pertaining to the specific game and realm are naturally learned through playing the video game itself. Thus the video gamer will naturally be giving the social cues appropriate to the video game, its players, and for social inclusivity.

There's a learning curve; the longer a video gamer plays a video game and interacts within the world, the better he or she will be able to communicate. A "newb" or newcomer to the virtual game knows very little about the video game landscape or environment; but will quickly become familiar and adapt as they process the new information. A new person usually has this type of designation within the game itself until they become familiar with the video game controls, atmosphere, and social cues. As they play through the game and learn the basic mechanics, eventually becoming more advanced, they shed this title and become included in social events, parties, and friendships. At this point, the video gamer is interacting with others under a new paradigm of social influence including the new social cues pertaining to the specific society.

This is akin to a traveler visiting a different country. After a period of time we acclimate to our surroundings in order to fit in; the video game realm is no different than this same concept. One needs to *experience* the world and learn from it in order to process, regulate, and incorporate it. While visiting a different country, we are lost. We don't speak the language, know the customs, or have any clue how to operate. Nevertheless, we observe, take notes, and slowly integrate ourselves into the general public. After a period of time it becomes much more difficult to tell the natives from the visitors. This is adaptation to the surroundings we are in. The relatability to video game culture and becoming immersed to new social cues is no different. The *adaption* may take time, but will occur with induction into the society, paying attention to the culture, and easily meeting requirements for what is considered to be normal for the beliefs of the population.

A second concern usually voiced by parents is "the people he/she plays with aren't even real friends." A more valid concern usually voiced in response is why the parents believe this is so. Just because the person a video gamer plays with isn't present in the room with him or her does not negate a possible friendship. The gamer usually has formed a bond with an individual, a group of individuals, or is part of a guild within the video game as discussed in Chapter Two.

Video gamers who are part of a guild are socially interacting and participating in an important relationship with others. By stating these relationships do not matter or that they are "not real" invalidates their experience. By invalidating the experience, in some form we are invalidating the video gamers themselves, **telling them they do not exist or matter.** Most parents and caregivers do not realize they are conducting themselves in this manner and usually are shocked when the concept is put into the previous terms. As an example, think about Facebook friends. How many of them have you met? Do you have communication with them every day? Every week? Could someone randomly pick one of the friends online and you have the ability to say you interact with them at least once a week in person? How many of your friends do you physically see on a regular basis? Why do these relationships matter more than a video gamer's? Most likely, a video gamer interacts more frequently and for longer periods of time with their video game friends than other people do through other mediums of technology today.

Guilds are a prime example of cohesion and individuals or video gamers forming bonds over similar ideas or goals. Although guilds are not the only method of companionship, friends, and allies one will find in the video game realm. There is additional global or online presence one has while playing the video game as their identity as a gamer. Through this connection, different acquaintances and approaching others do not appear to be as daunting anymore. While "stranger danger" is an important note to discuss with children as there are predators among the online social realm, this is not nearly as prevalent as popular media portrays. Through these interactions online, forming bonds and relationships with other video gamers allows the person to have less difficulty approaching others for help. The online interactions naturally teach life skills as they occur in-game. The larger difficulty problem is psychologically working with the individual to reach out with these known skills and make the connection to real world circumstances. Once this connection is made through an analytic interpretation with therapeutic implications, the child, adolescent, or adult puts the pieces together that their virtual world avatar is an integral and important part of them.

Clinical Case

My client Dean is a teenage boy in high school who was having difficulties reaching out to others, asking for help, and communicating with people in his school. Dean socially had a couple of friends at school, was having trouble in science, but mainly discussed the topic of video games in therapy sessions. In the virtual world he was a fearless conqueror of enemy bases, laying waste to rival lands with many individuals in his and other clans bowing to him. His friends in school were his companions and together they helped save the virtual lands from many different foes with Dean as their leader. Dean felt powerful and important in the game, but less so outside the game and in his school life. He was a shy and introverted adolescent with self-esteem issues when talking to others face-to-face; however, in the game, he was courageous, talked to everyone he could, was well-liked and respected, and a clan/guild leader. The difficulty lay with transferring his online self-esteem to his real life self.

It was fairly easy working with Dean to gain acceptance as I was familiar with his game of Elder Scrolls Online; a popular Massively Multiplayer Online game (MMO). After discussing his attributes and leadership skills for a couple weeks, we made the connection he felt inferior compared to his character in the game. His warrior character held a rich backstory: he was from a noble family, but cursed because an evil wizard had sapped his father's strength and taken over the kingdom. "Dean" was then forced to leave and told to never return. He was questing in the video game to end the evil sorcerer's grip on his kingdom with hopes of attaining great power and courage. With his companions, he was able to survive and accomplish feats impossible alone. This was a key point in working with him on the transferring of his character's qualities and archetypal elements on this real life experiences. This will be discussed more in Chapter Six.

Dean's in-game character had made choices he could only fantasize about and play through the character. This made him bold, daring, and even courageous because of the powers he attained by leveling up and working with his friends to defeat the virtual monsters. In a way, he was facing his personal fears through the virtual character and talents chosen, he just needed the analytical and psychological push to make the connection. Once made, he was able to realize the potential he had in the real world and began to incorporate his character's ideals and powers into his own self-concept.

Later in the sessions, he mentioned he was interested in a girl in his school but was unable to find the courage to ask her out. We discussed how he imagined his warrior would ask her out and he humbly replied "courtesy and treating her as a princess." We used imagery and role-playing to figure out what he could say when he approached her. I additionally suggested he use his companions to help with his ideas. Not surprisingly, a couple of weeks later, his mother mentioned he had been seeing a girl in his class on occasion during the week and appeared to be happier than before. When we discussed this in our weekly therapy session he blushed and admitted he had found the courage to ask her out. In fact, Dean related further he had talked to his teacher about his grades and, to her surprise, asked for extra help. He began seeing the teacher after school for tutoring. He additionally attributed his newfound confidence to asking his new girlfriend out on a date. He reported he would have never found the courage to ask for help without thinking about his character and the positive qualities found within himself.

Our work continues to this day and Dean, of course, still plays his character and we overlay the qualities of his warrior upon his own self to much success in other communication and personal relationship areas. He has many new friends, online and offline, which he keeps in touch with and has begun to show leadership qualities in his classroom, much to his mother's surprise and enjoyment. This is just one therapeutic story which can be told about adolescents and adults playing video games. These patients require a different thinking structure and approach to the topics of video gaming combining both academic writing and community practice: an avenue missing from either side independently. This extra curiosity and work results in expansive growth potential for video gamers who seek therapy or guidance from academics, their families, and therapists.

Technology Avatars

Sherry Turkle, a well-known MIT professor, promoted the idea that technology could in fact help individuals collaborate and explore themselves across virtual spaces. Her writings indicate that people become liberated when they use online avatars and technology as modes and models to communicate. A *liberation of the self* is what it is commonly called when discussing this idea of the postmodern self. Liberation of the self is thought to mean the individual who is being liberated, in this case through the playing of online avatars, is freed from physical embodiment and allowed to reinvent themselves through the different technological spectrums. In her book, *The Second Self* (2010), she interviews a variety of individuals who use and are associated with computers and online games or simulations. Through the interviews, it is revealed that individuals who use technology experience them as both an extension of the self and part of the external world outside of their body. A common example of this is a smart phone. The smart phone is used to talk to people across virtual spaces (e.g. Twitter, Facebook, etc.), promoting a type of extended self, through the Social Networking Site (SNS) mediums, but also simultaneously consciously and unconsciously recognized that the object used, the phone, is an object outside of the individual self, thus, a tool which is to be used mechanically as originally created. Individuals ultimately recognize that it is not part of us physically, but at the same time, part of everyday rituals and appearances which are representations of who we are or the individual's self-concept. The phone becomes an avatar for people to use and talk to others socially across SNSs.

The core composition of an avatar is quite simple. It is made up of pixels, has a name, picture, clothes, interaction qualities, sometimes spells or melee attacks, and can be seen as a social representation of the player. The character may have been created through pixels, but a story develops surrounding the character, what they may represent, and what their overall missions and motivations are. As Mark Meadows (2007) put it in his book *I, Avatar* "ultimately, avatars are about the advancement of personality within a kind of fiction that is both social and personal" (pg. 23). By creating an avatar and engaging with other players or even NPCs in some cases, a fiction and documentation of one's life through the avatar is created which can be shared with others.

Using the ideas behind liberating the self and avatars, there is a case made for all SNS to be considered interactive spaces which are representations of the self. Social media sites like Facebook and Twitter *are avatar based multiuser environments* similar to role playing games, there is just more user input into the creation of the individual avatars because they are based more upon the person using them rather than being pre-programmed by a programmer. This allows more freedom in avatar choices and interactions instead of them being confined through programming interactions. The SNSs become objects to which one experiences and interacts within a network framework of the self and objects which has "multiplexity," existing in complex relationships with one another, and "multispatiality," existing in multiple spaces including physical, virtual, and digital at the same time.

Jaime Banks (2015) suggests relationships between objects continually exist in complex webs or relationships and through the intermingling relationships meaning emerges as we interact with them. By interacting with the different objects and relationships found in everyday life we create the meaning which we live by. Banks further iterates "what seems to be vast, complex phenomena are reframed as networks of objects that hang together through both material and semiotic connections across spaces" (pg. 13). Through the vast connections of technology, video games, and SNSs individuals are able to create and even further our understanding of meaning and relationship values. In essence, through the creation and manipulation of avatars, we create meaning, relationships, and a place for new thought to birth.

Avatars and Object Relations(hips)

Object Relations theory is a form of psychoanalytic psychology focusing on the development of psyche in individuals during childhood through adolescence (Greenberg & Mitchell, 2003; Klein, Bernard, & Singer, 1992). Psyche is defined as the mind, soul, persona, mental or psychological structure of a person and how they interact and are motivated in the world. The manner in which individuals relate to one another stems from their childhood experiences and is perpetuated through experience from childhood to adolescence into adulthood. A common example of thought in Object Relations theory is that if an individual who was severely abused as a child, he/she will grow up believing that experienced relationship is a primary manner in which to relate to one another. The person who experienced the trauma would expect similar behaviors from others whom they grow closer to. They may even be drawn towards other people intimately who exhibit abusive behaviors because the traumatized believe it to be a crucial and comfortable form of love.

When first born, neonates have to differentiate between themselves, others, and their environment. This is done through interacting with the milieu, other people and things, and with enough time. After a period, usually when a baby begins to smile and become more aware of their surroundings, they realize they are not the only object in this world (Greenberg & Mitchell, 2003; Klein, Bernard, & Singer, 1992). They have begun to differentiate. From this point, they create one or two primary objects dependent upon their caregivers, a mom and dad object, a mom object, a dad object, two mom objects, or two dad objects as examples. The child distinguishes there are other objects besides their own self. The primary objects created in childhood continue to grow with more and more time eventually becoming the driving force of a child's mannerisms and interactions in the world.

During the childhood into adolescence stages, the primary objects have good and bad qualities and the child learns what these are, based upon their behaviors, encouragements, punishments, rewards, and so on. This helps to shape their world and define characteristics such as what it means to be loved, good, and bad. Based upon the interactions with the parents, whether good or bad, the child will hold onto this form of interaction as a basis for being accepted or rejected from another person (Greenberg & Mitchell, 2003; Klein, Bernard, & Singer, 1992). As they child grows, the primary objects will split because they do not fit into the same object that the caregivers have and a new one will have to be created. An example of this is when they first go to school or a daycare, they are introduced to many new people including teachers. They may test out the new guardian or friends with behaviors which may or may not be approved and accepted at home in an attempt to assess where the new individuals fits into the object scheme. When the new individual does not fit into the system or object that has already been created (e.g. the mother or father object) it can be called a splitting of the original object. The original object does not die or disappear, but stays the same. In the end a new object has been born aside from the other one to make sense of this new person. This is how we create new objects throughout life, by the fracturing of the old ones to make room for the new.

Avatars are another form of interactional and interjected objects that are used in a similar sense as described above. They create splits depending upon the relationship forged in the interactions. As an example, this happen often when politics are involved due to the polarizing nature of the topic. It becomes easy to place individuals into a box and label them bad, incorrect, right, wrong, or accurate. From this point of labeling the individual avatar we are left with the decision of what to do about it. Do we listen further in attempt to understand the situation? Do we throw them to the side and defriend them? Do we attempt to strike up a conversation and try to find a sliver of similarity? The consequential actions, behaviors, and outcomes are what individuals need to focus on instead of the opinionated disagreement. Lacking a common ground or attempt at understanding the other creates a barrier to the conversation and can be seen as the equivalent of banging one's head into a wall trying to force their opinion through. Obviously with communication through online domains, attempts at trying to find common ground will take more effort and are not impossible. This is what makes video gamers so adept at online communication, they have more practice with it through their video game play. While playing the video game, the gamer is actually communicating and interacting with their avatar intimately. They care whether they live or die, finish or fail, help or hurt, etc.

Video game avatars provide an object, both bad and good as defined by the programmer and discovered through the storyline. They teach what commonly and societally is taught rule and law wise. The difference is the video gamer has the opportunity to play against, or even in some cases for, the negative nature of the villain. This opportunity to reveal the storyline and play as a character for good or evil has powerful implications for the gamer. The simple good versus evil storyline is not the only one which can be used. Take the therapeutic story outlined above, the individual character that is played is an object which the player has a relationship with. Dean's warrior was powerful in the game and the object he represented for Dean allowed him access to different innate abilities he had, but was too shy to use. He was looked at as not just a warrior, but a leader as well. The warrior was a good object for him to help him discover a different part of himself which may have been hidden. Discussing it in our sessions allowed him to overwrite the bad object that he was not worthy of personal and intimate interactions outside of the video game.

Qualities that are inherent in the character can be extrapolated and used in the therapy session to internally motivate the client. Friends made and found in the game can also provide similar assets: becoming a leader, having people look to others for guidance, using powerful influence appropriately, talking to others, feeling important. What are even more powerful are some of the main characters found in video games who seem to survive against all odds. The connections made to them are deeply powerful as they appear stoic and resourceful, ready to take on any danger thrown at them. Master Chief of the Halo games is one which exhibits these qualities. The player is the Master Chief in the game and has to battle against hordes of opponents which easily outnumber him, and has to survive catastrophic events which would normally kill anyone; and in most cases do to lesser people in the storyline. Isaac Clarke in the Dead Space horror series has a similar battle against an undead form of being. Isaac's ability to be resourceful and engage power stations back online while battling literal death coming at him is admirable to anyone willing to uncover his traumatic storyline. Link in The Legend of Zelda is an orphan who travels Hyrule to discover he is the savior of the realm even though throughout his short life he is shunned as an outsider. Video gamers have grown to love these characters for qualities they also have: resourcefulness in the face of adversity, being able to battle back from insurmountable odds, saving yourself, being an outsider, but still having a purpose. These objects are powerful illustrations of what we can do in life if we are able to harness our internal resources appropriately. It just requires the thoughtful eye and ear of the psychologist or mental health expert, and most importantly a willingness to explore the fantasy with the video gamer, to discover what the object means to them.

References

Banks, J. (2015). Multimodal, multiplex, multispatial: A network model of the self. *New Media and Society, 19*(3), 419–438.

Castells, M. (1996). *The rise of the network society*. Malden, MA: Blackwell Publishers.

Ess, C., & Sudweeks, F. (2001). *Culture, technology, communication: Towards an intercultural global village*. Albany, NY: State University of New York Press.

Greenberg, J. R., & Mitchell, S. A. (2003). *Object relations in psychoanalytic theory*. Cambridge, MA: Harvard University Press.

Griffin, E. A. (2011). *A first look at communication theory*. Boston, MA: McGraw-Hill.

Jones, S. (1998). *CyberSociety 2.0: Revisiting computer-mediated communication and community*. Thousand Oaks, CA: Sage Publications.

Klein, R. H., Bernard, H. S., & Singer, D. L. (1992). *Handbook of contemporary group psychotherapy: Contributions from object relations, self psychology, and social systems theories*. Madison, CT: International Universities Press.

Meadows, M. S. (2007). *I, avatar: The culture and consequences of having a second life*. Indianapolis, IN: New Riders.

Sherif, C. W. (1963). Social categorization as a function of latitude of acceptance and series range. *The Journal of Abnormal and Social Psychology, 67*(2), 148–156.

Sherif, C. W., Sherif, M., Nebergall, R. E. (1965). *Attitude and attitude change: The social judgment-involvement approach.* Philadelphia, PA: Saunders.

Thurlow, C., Tomic, A., & Lengel, L. B. (2004). *Computer mediated communication: Social interaction and the Internet.* London: SAGE.

Turkle, S. (2010). *The second self: Computers and the human spirit.* Cambridge, MA: MIT Press.

Weiten, W., Dunn, D., & Hammer, E. Y. (2015). *Psychology applied to modern life: Adjustment in the 21st century.* Stamford, CT: Cengage Learning.

Wright, K. B., & Webb, L. M. (2011). *Computer-mediated communication in personal relationships.* New York: Peter Lang.

Society and Video Games

5

Video games have been a normalized function of entertainment since the arrival of the Nintendo Entertainment System in 1985 (Sheff, 1999). Since then, many new games, ideas, virtual worlds, and consoles have emerged in multiple forms that have catered to the gamer. Through the virtual worlds that have been created by the video game industry, individuals have been able to immerse themselves in various social interactions, different environments, and play as different characters (Bartle, 2003; 2004).

The Entertainment Software Association (ESA, 2017) is a main research entity of video games, video gamers, and playability throughout the United States. The ESA reports essential facts about the computer and video game industry in their yearly research review. Recently, the ESA reported that 67% of all United States households own a device that is used to play video games, while 65% are home to at least one person who plays video games at least three hours per week. The average video gamer is 35 years old, and women aged 18 years or older now represent a significantly greater proportion of the game playing base than males under the age of 18. Over half of the videogames played by video gamers are multiplayer games, suggesting that playing with others is a large motivational form of video game entertainment. Furthermore, 90% of parents are with their children when they purchase video games, and 67% of parents play video games with their children at least once per week. Other research reports have stated that 97% of individuals aged 12–17 play a form of video games across the multitude of video game devices (Lenhart et al., 2008). It is clear, at this point in time, that video games are a definitive part of society and are intertwined into everyday life.

Research into video games, and the utilization across different areas and environments, shows video games have positive effects on individuals, serving a wide range of emotional needs along with intellectual stimulation (Granic, Lobel, & Engels, 2013; Kato, 2010; Redd et al., 1987; Turkle, 1994; Vasterling, Jenkins, Tope, & Burish, 1993). Olson (2010) found youths who played video games were better able to express creativity, had increased social and intellectual curiosity, and a larger focus to discover the real world compared to youth who did not play video games. Within the medical field, video games have been shown to help with the engagement of patients, pain management for chemotherapy treatments, and prevention of certain asthma attacks (Kato, 2010; Redd et al., 1987; Vasterling, Jenkins, Tope, & Burish, 1993). Furthermore, video games are currently being used in some mental health settings and have resulted in clients being more cooperative and enthusiastic about psychotherapy (Kato, 2010). Finally, video games have been utilized in education to increase grades, learning, reading, and the ability to work with abstract ideas (Gee, 2007; Koster, 2005; Squire & Barab, 2004). However, even with these benefits, there are still concerns that video games are the cause of violence and aggression in youth and adults.

The Video Game Violence Debate

Whether violence within video games has a negative impact or influences behavior, and to what degree, has generated global discussion (Australian Government, Attorney General's Department, 2010, p. 32; Brown v. EMA, 2011). There has been a significant interest in whether or not video game playing impacts moral behavior, aggression, and criminal activity. The debate is centered on the notion that what gamers are exposed to, and are able to do within video games, desensitizes them to the same experiences in real life situations, thereby opening up the immoral capacity to create similar crimes based upon their in-game actions.

Due to the interactive nature of videogames and the potential of engaging in activities in a virtual environment that would be deemed otherwise unacceptable in the real world, some researchers suggest video games promote and encourage anti-social behavior. Extensive research has investigated whether exposure to such themes found in violent video games (e.g., violence, sex, and drug use) promotes the wrong message—that these kind of negative behaviors are considered acceptable (Anderson & Bushman, 2001; Anderson & Dill, 2000; Arriaga et al., 2006; Dill & Dill, 1998; Funk, Buchman, Jenks, & Bechtoldt, 2003; Huesmann, 2007). Although these studies suggest that the messages portrayed within the virtual worlds are causing harm, these studies have also been questioned for their seeming lack of similar conditions to playing video games, the research methods used, and the variables chosen for study (Ferguson, 2007; 2013; 2014). While there is considerable research investigating the negative effects associated with children playing violent video games, there is also substantial research asserting a lack of conclusive evidence to support the connection between aggression in video gamers and their engagement with violent video game content (Bean & Groth-Marnat, 2014; Brown v. EMA, 2011; Ferguson, 2007; 2013; Markey & Markey, 2010; Olson, 2010).

The other side of the research arena suggests that video games do not cause aggression, or that the previous research conclusions are spurious at best as the result of poor research methodologies and inconclusive results. In fact, the phrase "correlation does not necessarily mean causation" is one that is commonly used by researchers of this area; pro-aggression research has presumptuously relied upon correlational research to infer their findings (Bean & Groth-Marnat, 2014; Brown v. EMA, 2011; Ferguson, 2007; 2013; Markey & Markey, 2010; Olson, 2010)

As a direct result of these investigations there has been a significant increase in research surrounding the effects of video games and those who play them. While many individuals are familiar with the debate of video games and aggressive behaviors, other areas of investigation have sprung up due to an increase of research interest. These new areas (i.e. addiction, social ineptness, mental health etc.) have additionally gathered much focus upon whether video games cause these "new" problems to arise. However, what is commonly forgotten is that these problems, which have plagued society, were present before the introduction and increasing playability of video games. The concerns become more pronounced due to a more visible medium being present in society, but are further expressed through the idea of moral panic.

In the United States the arguments of video game violence and aggression climaxed in a Supreme Court landmark case of whether California had the right to ban the sale of certain violent video games to customers based upon age. California made their case that by consuming violent video games children were becoming more violent, desensitized to violence, and destructive within society. The concerns stemmed from school violence, shootings, and the belief that minors who play violent video games would be influenced by the violence and become violent themselves. However, they were alternatively using particular research which tailored to their concerns and were being societally pushed by activist groups which were against the concept of video games (e.g. the Parents Television Council, 2011).

For instance, information cited as the main reason for the concern came from a minority of researchers and was not inclusive of the entire field of video game violence study suggesting a form of publication bias. The entirety of the research presented did not support the purported suggestion that playing violent video games causes aggression and violence. Furthermore, the studies cited were criticized for their methods of measuring aggression (Brown v. EMA, 2011; Ferguson, 2007). In one study aggression was measured through sending loud noises through speakers with the competition component of pressing a button first. The individual who pressed the button first was able to set the volume and duration of a loud noise to their opponent, who in fact was non-existent, as a punishment (Anderson & Dill, 2000). In another study participants were asked to complete a word task following violent video game play where the player finishing filling in a partially completed word with the first word that pops into their head. For instance, if the word needing completion was KI_ _ and the video gamer wrote KILL instead of another word such as KISS they were considered to be aggressive. These types of methodologies were the basis of explanations for why playing violent video games cause violent behavior. It is difficult to see the connection established by these studies when there is not a true act of violence or aggression being committed (Anderson et al., 2004; Sestir & Bartholow, 2010).

Ultimately, Brown vs. EMA resulted in a ruling stating video games enjoy full speech protection from the Constitution (Brown v. EMA, 2011). Additionally, the Supreme Court raised concerns about the state of video game research. They cited methodological flaws, publication bias, and only correlational findings, which are not considered to lead to causation, found within the literature reviewed. Researchers within the area of violent video games have similarly had difficulties with the reported conclusiveness of the research citing authorship bias, confounded methodologies, validity of aggression measures, and possible moral panic agendas (Ferguson, 2007; 2013).

Many more scientific studies have evaluated whether playing video games has a causal relationship with violence and violent acts. A majority of the research currently acknowledges a short and small increase in aggressive tendencies after playing video games, but also recognize that these aggressive tendencies are short-term and do not have any long-term impact upon video gamers. In fact, these studies have led a majority of researchers to conclude that no significant links between video games and aggression exist; they do not support the notion of banning them or the concern that these games cause video gamers to become violent or aggressive.

Data supporting the rise of criminal activities and consumption of violent video games has also not been supported. Chris Ferguson's seminal paper in *The American Psychologist*, Violent Video Games and the Supreme Court (2013), pinpoints that with the rise of violent video game sales there has been a significant decrease in youth violence. Ferguson notes through his research that over the past 40 years of youth violence there has been a decline of violence involving youth, but at the same time there has been a significant increase in the development and consumption of violent video games. This curious bit of data can be seen as a conundrum for those believing that playing violent video games causes aggression and violence. The opposite should have been apparent. It is important to note that this is a correlational relationship as well, and abides by the same cause and effect principles as previously stated, but as another well-known researcher Rachel Kowert (2016, pg, 30) detailed—"Rather, the findings indicate the unlikelihood that violent video games play actively contributes to an increase in youth violence." Furthermore, another study by Bean & Ferro (2016) suggests, through pre and post aggression scores with violent video games as a moderator, that pre-state aggression scores are more indicative of post-state aggression than the violent video game itself. Overall, it appears that, even with violent video games being played, they may not even moderate aggression and what research may want to pay attention to is other areas of pre-state aggression rather than video games as a moderator variable.

Even with both sides of the debate continuing today, the American Psychological Association (APA) has claimed on two accounts a determination that violent video games cause aggression and negative effects in children, youths, and adults. Within their latest review of the literature the APA has acknowledged that multiple factors exist which lead an individual to become aggressive or violent, but continue to assert that violent video games are one of the risk factors (APA, 2015). While this is a progression from their previous statement, it is still concerning for researchers in the area of violent video games, as more evidence accumulates against the same consensus made by the APA.

Moral Panic

Stanley Cohen first coined and introduced Moral Panic Theory in 1972. He asserted that there was an epidemic occurring which needed to be controlled or subdued. These trepidations have always plagued researchers and lawmakers alike, due to the wildfire-like-state the concern creates in the public eye through the spread of misinformation or fear-based mentalities. The anxieties carelessly create havoc and intense emotions within a societal presence clamoring for justice or an entity to save them from what is feared. The major concern with this mentality is that not much information is known about the distressing problem or the effects of it, which adds an additional layer of fear upon the already intensified concern. In essence, the problem is easily overshadowed by the monstrosity of the public fear of it, creating an unequal balance of how to deal with the problem. Moral panic additionally has the power to create a hive-mind mentality in which mass behavior against the concern is fueled by the moral panic.

The concern of the epidemic occurs when there is enough of an apprehension risen about a problem through narrated information, or even the simple recitation of facts, resulting in an overblown fear mongering of a perceived scapegoat. Cohen (1972) stated moral panics occur when an identified condition, episode, person, or group of people emerge to be considered a threat to societal values becoming what he called "folk devils" as they are perceived to supposedly threaten the social order. The moral panic can focus upon anything or anyone at any time, but usually occurs when there is more of a psychological phenomenon or craze which not much information may be known about or there is a spread of misinformation. There have been many moral panics throughout the existence of man from witch hunts, religious persecution, to the war on drugs in America.

Cohen proposed that moral panics have five key stages:

1. Someone, something, or a group are considered to be a threat to social norms or general community interests
2. The threat is depicted as a simple and recognizable form or symbol for easy recognition by the media
3. The portrayal and information about the form or symbol rouses public concerns creating an uneasy tension
4. There is a response from recognized authorities and policy makers to help quell the fear
5. The moral panic issues result in societal change

Moral panics tend to focus on youths, youth behavior, concerns, or perceived risks to well-being (Cohen, 1972; Goode & Ben-Yehuda, 2009; Markey & Ferguson, 2017). It comes out of a worry for a specific group of individuals (i.e. women, the poor, video gamers) and usually has noble intentions, but

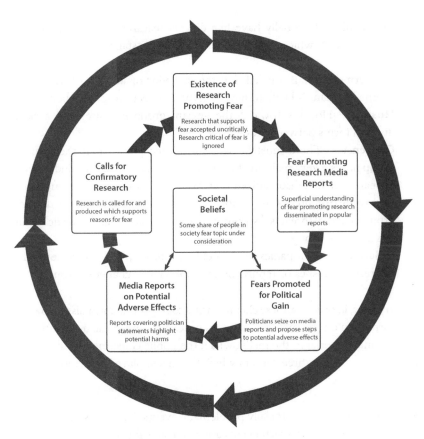

Figure 5.1 Moral Panic Theory

Artwork by Christopher Ferguson, used with permission

implementation is significantly problematic. An example of this would be in the early 1990s the societal fear resulting in a moral panic that children were being kidnapped by satanic cults and sexually abused while being integrated into satanic rituals. The fears spread even further through society creating false memories and testimony of children reporting experiences with satanic cults whom did not actually have any involvement with them. These occurrences created a sense of panic within society with many individuals being jailed and defamed throughout the process of it only later to be acquitted of the charges. However, the damage was already completed and many lives were changed for the worse. A moral panic can focus upon anything in existence and usually focuses on a new and not completely understood phenomenon. Society is not known for handling these moral panic cases well.

Moral panics additionally have five distinct features as distinguished by Ben-Yehuda (2009) which take place within Cohen's stages:

- **Concern**—There is a belief that the behavior or activity of the group deemed deviant is likely to have a negative effect on societal beliefs.
- **Hostility**—Hostility towards the deviant group increases and a clear division forms between "them" and "us."
- **Consensus**—There must be widespread acceptance that the deviant group poses a very real threat to society and that the deviant individuals appear weak and disorganized towards the other portioned group.
- **Disproportionality**—The action or actions taken against the deviant group or actual threat is disproportionate to the actual and realistic threat posed by the group.
- **Volatility**—Moral panics tend to ebb and flow quickly because public interest diminishes or reports on the moral panic changes narrative.

However, in order for these characteristics to be prominent, a dissemination of information on the rhetoric has to occur. Cohen linked the distribution of moral panic material to the media which the public consumes regularly. He believed there were three roles in which the media played a part in creation of a moral panic:

1. Selecting deviant or socially problematic events deemed as newsworthy and then selecting which events are candidates for the story.
2. The transmission of the claims using images and rhetoric of moral panics.
3. Making an overall claim based upon their chosen story or data.

Cohen further argued that any form of media can be linked to the volatility of creating a moral panic while labeling action and people into polarizing groups.

Cohen's reasoning was if individuals are reading the newspapers, watching the nightly news, or listening to the radio newscast, they are consuming what is being told to them. While this may be deemed normal, one must be aware that within 30 minutes of airtime, or within an entire newspaper, there can only be so much information divulged. Therefore, it is common practice for the news media to only report will sell their copies or subscriptions. This on more than one occasion includes selecting stories deemed as being newsworthy and then reporting upon them with a selection of information. The individuals consuming this material are then led to believe that they have heard the entire story and consensus of material, when that rarely occurs. Cohen believed that this was a large reason why moral panics occur so easily.

As stated in Bean et al. (2017, pg. 7), "Predetermined beliefs ultimately incentivize scholars, politicians and news media to make public claims supporting the moral panic. Moral panics most often decline when the audience does." This leads one familiar with moral panic to believe that there is more information than one is being told. With moral panics inciting a lot of concern and call for actions, they place significant pressures upon scientists, lawmakers, and politicians to combat the concern, leading to presumptuous allegations and policies, which in fact usually do more harm than good.

When appropriate curtailing research is not conducted, society falls into the trap of moral panic and impulsively acts upon their concerns. There are examples of this throughout history with not just video games, but other items as well. For instance, in the 1950's it was switchblades causing panic, in the 1970's the war on drugs, the 1980's Dungeons and Dragons, and even today video games and violence are still in the public eye (Markey & Ferguson, 2017). What society knows now is that these concerns were based upon ill-conceived notions and acted upon without appropriate information. In essence, it is good to always conduct personal research about a topic or become more familiar with it in order to combat these difficulties. The following are prime samples of how moral panic caused more harm than good.

Pinball

In an editorial by John Teti (2010) about pinball in the city of New York moral panic struck again in the 1940s. Teti explained that the mayor at the time, Fiorello LaGuardia, had been successfully eradicating crime bosses in New York. He was reported to have a significant power base which helped him win three elections, but premised upon his populist appeal of making New York a safer place. He would tout his accomplishments to the public to continue winning their favor and securing his place as mayor.

This led to LaGuardia claiming pinball games were a form of gambling which entitles them to be banned during the 1930's. He accused pinball of stealing money, being used by mobsters for money, that they were a form of gambling, and he did so while on a public broadcast knowing he would grab the attention of the public. While there was some truth, that the mob did have pinball tables, it was and still is unclear how much shadiness actually ensued. Regardless, LaGuardia damned them anyways.

The public latched onto the story and fell for what LaGuardia was telling them. LaGuardia even went as far as to label pinball machines "games of chance" allowing him to ban them more easily under current law statutes at the time. There were instances of LaGuardia and Commissioner Valentine smashing confiscated pinball machines, claiming they were saving the city from a disastrous form of gambling (Teti, 2010). World War II came about and gave him further ammo—literally. He claimed that the balls being used in pinball machines could be melted down and sent to the troops, using this new rhetoric to repeat his attack and fire up his fan base. It worked. He was able to confiscate over 3,000 pinball machines for destruction in just a few months' time. The incident even drew in the city's courts, who eventually sided with LaGuardia.

Eventually, however, pinball was reinstated within the city limits due to Roger Sharpe, now considered to be one of the world's expert on pinball machines. He brought evidence to the city showing that individuals who played the game for extended periods of time actually increased their abilities for the game and he was even brought in as a court expert on the matter. Sharpe was able to showcase the needed information which was backed up by evidence to dissuade the then misinformed population and city officials who had pinball banned. Sharpe can be considered to be the main reason why the moral panic on pinball does not exist any longer (Teti. 2010).

Columbine High School Massacre

One of the most well-known incidents spurring societal moral panic was the Columbine High School Massacre. It occurred on April 20th, 1999 in Colorado and was carried out by two students, Eric Harris and Dylan Klebold (Brooks, 2004; James, 2009; History, 2017). The two students of the high school were avid players of the video game Doom to the degree they even came up with their own levels to play. Their attack on the school had multiple complex and highly planned variables including a fire bomb to divert firefighters, and other homemade bombs placed in the school's cafeteria to assert their power within the situation. In the end, the two students murdered 12 students and one teacher in their massacre.

The massacre sparked many moral panic debates due to the multitude of variables that came forth as the investigation progressed. In total, nine moral panics stemmed from this event: gun control laws, bullying, school security, high school cliques, gun culture, Goth culture, antidepressants, teenage internet use, and violence in video games (Brooks, 2004; Cullen, 2016; Goldberg, 1999; James, 2009; History, 2017).

The overall motivations of the shootings were never fully identified, but certain factors were reported to have sparked the shooting, such as mental health difficulties and access to firearms. The aspect of whether the killers had created and used video games to simulate the shooting beforehand has never been substantiated. Regardless, the moral panics began as soon as information was reported about why the shooters may have committed their shooting. The end result was a report which was published by the FBI concluding that the mental health of the individuals was the primary culprit and motivation behind the shootings. Harris was labeled a "clinical psychopath" while Klebold a "depressive" (Cullen, 2004; 2016; Klebold, 2017). Furthermore, there was significant evidence that the two students had planned this attack for over a year, a fact that was documented in their journals (Cullen, 2004; 2016; Goldberg, 1999; James, 2009). However, this report was published five years after the incident, a timeline which was not kind to the moral panic agenda and caused many parents, schools, researchers, and law makers to believe there was more to the issue than reported by the FBI.

Sandy Hook Massacre

Adam Lanza shocked the world when he murdered 20 children and six teachers at Sandy Hook Elementary in Connecticut. Lanza was portrayed as a young man who had some difficulties in life but was obsessed with violent video games. (Bates & Pow, 2013; State of Connecticut, 2013). His online killing record, including headshots to online avatars posted as a "descent into madness and murder." The media jumped at this news and the moral panic from Columbine arose again that Lanza trained himself to kill using online violent video games. From the earlier fallacy that Lanza must have been influenced by his video game play, lawmakers attempted again to ban violent video games citing they were the reason Lanza completed his massacre.

Later the following year, the report on the incident was made public by the State of Connecticut. It showed an individual who had some difficulties with social settings, loud noises, and confusion. He was homeschooled for a period of time and considered a loner by some. However, Lanza was also called creative and imaginative by some of his observers. He was later diagnosed with Asperger's Disorder, a disorder which is now subsumed under Autism Spectrum Disorder in the current DSM-5. His mother and mental health professionals commented that they did not observe any characteristics which would have been indicative of his future behavior (State of Connecticut, 2013).

Ultimately, the report suggested that mental health or video games were not indicative of Lanza committing the crimes, even though he was reported to have mental health issues, and the police found him to have planned his crimes intentionally. Furthermore, when his video game habits were researched, it did show that he played some violent video games, but they were not his favorite. His favorite video game he played was called Dance Dance Revolution, which is a fitness game having no violence in it at all (Ferguson, 2014; State of Connecticut, 2013). This game was cited to be his most played, clearly not backing up the claim that violent video games were the reason for the murders.

Does Playing Monopoly Make You a Millionaire?

Moral panic can cause much harm and dismay when the masses grab onto rhetoric and do not think critically about the claims. This is apparent with the violence and video game debate, the past incidents within the United States, and with poor research and biased conclusions. It is important to think critically about many of the claims today surrounding video games: the beliefs that video games cause individuals to be aggressive or violent; that gamers are loners with no social skills; or are even addicted to their games. Research has not been able to support these claims and yet they still exist. This is the power of Moral Panic. Does that mean by playing the game of Monopoly one will become a millionaire?

By critically analyzing research being reported or consumed by others, one becomes a more informed consumer of knowledge. Indeed, most headlines today are taglines for advertising clicks rather than proclaiming important knowledge. In some cases, a reader has to dig for the information or the actual case study being presented amidst ads. Many online sources regurgitate another story, slightly changing it without appropriately checking references and then publishing it without a second thought. This leads to misinformation about studies, research, and science which is of importance to the public.

As an example, imagine a study which utilized a research approach of studying video gamers, those who play often each week, and non-video gamers, those who rarely play. The researchers use an MRI to take images of their brains before and after playing video games for a month. They notice in the non-video gamer's brains a shrinkage of grey matter of three percent after playing the video game. The researchers then claim that playing video games reduces grey matter in individuals and receive invitations from local news and blogs about their study. The researchers state the same idea about how their study discovered this important finding without discussing any of the minute details of the study. Seems fishy right? What is not being told is the sample size, hours played per the month, style of play, research set up, types of games, where they played, who they played with, and so on. There are many more variables which are of importance to discuss, but the point is clear, not enough information has been delivered to make an accurate judgment upon the research.

This is what usually occurs with studies which make grand claims about their findings. It is important to not focus on the glamour of the results of research, but to be clear about how they may be impactful. For the example above, what if the three percent decrease was a correlation? It would impact the results in a more important manner as three percent is usually not a clear delineation and usually falls within the margin for error making the finding insignificant. To be clear, not all findings are displayed like this example, but enough are to bring about scientific worry. However, it is important not to get drawn into the hyperbole of what the tag line of a story says, but research the original source yourself, otherwise, we would all be millionaires by playing Monopoly, according to behavioral research.

References

American Psychological Association (APA) 2015. APA review confirms link between playing violent video games and aggression. Retrieved from www.apa.org/news/press/releases/2015/08/violent-video-games.aspx.

Anderson, C. A., & Bushman, B. J. (2001). Effects of violent video games on aggressive behavior, aggressive cognition, aggressive affect, physiological arousal, and prosocial behavior: A meta-analytic review of the scientific literature. *Psychological Science, 12*(5), 353–359.

Anderson, C.A., Carnagey, N.L., Flanagan, M., Benjamin, A.J., Eubanks, J., & Valentine, J.C. (2004). Violent videogames: Specific effects of violent content on aggressive thoughts and behavior. In: M. Zanna (Ed.) *Advances in experimental social psychology* (pp. 119–249). New York: Elsevier.

Anderson, C. A., & Dill, K. E. (2000). Video games and aggressive thoughts, feelings, and behavior in the laboratory and in life. *Journal of Personality and Social Psychology, 78,* 4, 772–790.

Arriaga, P., Esteves, F., Carneiro, P., & Monteiro, M. B. (2006). Violent computer games and their effects on state hostility and physiological arousal. *Aggressive Behavior, 32*(4), 358–371.

Australian Government, Attorney-General's Department. (2010). *Literature review on the impact of playing violent video games on aggression.* Barton, Australian Capital Territory, Australia: Commonwealth of Australia. Retrieved from www.apa.org/divisions/div46/articles.html.

Bartle, R. A. (2003). Hearts, clubs, diamonds, spades: players who suit MUDs. In K. Salen & E. Zimmerman, (Eds). *The game design reader: A rules of play anthology* (p. 754–787). Cambridge, MA: MIT Press.

Bartle, R. A. (2004). *Designing virtual worlds.* Berkeley, CA: New Riders.

Bates, D., & Pow, H. (2013). Lanza's descent to madness and murder: Sandy Hook shooter notched up 83,000 online kills including 22,000 'head shots' using violent games to train himself for his massacre. *Daily Mail.* Retrieved from www.dailymail.co.uk/news/article-2516427/SandyHook-shooter-Adam-Lanza-83k-online-kills-massacre.html.

Bean, A., & Groth-Marnat, G. (2014, March 10). Video gamers and personality: A five-factor model to understand game playing style. *Psychology of Popular Media Culture.* Advance online publication. http://dx.doi.org/10.1037/ppm0000025.

Bean, A. M., & Ferro, L. (2016). Predictors of Video Game Console Aggression. *Revista Argentina De Ciencias Del Comportamiento, 8*, 1.

Bean, A. M., Nielsen, R. K. L., van, R. A. J., & Ferguson, C. J. (2017). Video Game Addiction: The Push to Pathologize Video Games. *Professional Psychology: Research and Practice, 48*(5), 378–389,

Ben-Yehuda, N. (2009). Moral panics—36 years on. *British Journal of Criminology, 49*, 1–3. http://dx.doi.org/10.1093/bjc/azn076

Brooks, D. (2004). The Columbine Killers. *New York Times.* Retrieved from www.nytimes.com/2004/04/24/opinion/the-columbine-killers.html.

Brown v. Entertainment Merchants Association (Brown v. EMA), 131 S. Ct. 2729 (2011). Retrieved from www.supremecourt.gov/opinions/10pdf/08-1448.pdf.

Cohen, S. (1972). *Folk devils and moral panics: The creation of the Mods and Rockers.* London: Routledge

Cullen, D. (2004). The Depressive and the Psychopath. *Slate.* Retrieved from www.slate.com/articles/news_and_politics/assessment/2004/04/the_depressive_and_the_psychopath.html.

Cullen, D. (2016). *Columbine.* New York: Twelve Books.

Dill, K. E., & Dill, J. C. (1998). Video game violence: A review of the empirical literature. *Aggression and Violent Behavior, 3*(4), 407–428.

Entertainment Software Association (ESA). (2017). Essential facts about the computer and video game industry. Retrieved from: www.theesa.com/.

Ferguson, C. J. (2007). Evidence for publication bias in video game violence effects literature: A meta-analytic review. *Aggression and Violent Behavior, 12*, 470–482.

Ferguson, C. J. (2013). Violent video games and the Supreme Court: Lesson for the scientific community in the wake of the Brown v. Entertainment Merchants Association. *American Psychologist, 68*, 57–74. DOI: 10.1037/a0030597.

Ferguson, C. (2014). Lanza's Violent Video Game Play Overblown. Retrieved from www.courant.com/opinion/hc-op-ferguson-violent-video-games-blamessless-for-20140103-story.html.

Funk, J. B., Buchman, D. D., Jenks, J., & Bechtoldt, H. (2003). Playing violent video games, desensitization, and moral evaluation in children. *Journal of Applied Developmental Psychology, 24*(4), 413–436.

Gee, J. P. (2007). *Good video games plus good learning.* New York: Peter Lang.

Goldberg, C. (1999). Terror in Littleton: The shunned; For those who dress differently, an increase in being viewed as abnormal. *New York Times.* Retrieved from www.nytimes.com/1999/05/01/us/terror-littleton-shunned-for-those-who-dress-differentlyincrease-being-viewed.html.

Goode, E., & Ben-Yehuda, N. (2009). *Moral panics: The social construction of deviance,* 2nd Edition.

Granic, I., Lobel, A., & Engels, R. C. M. E. (2013). The benefits of playing video games. *American Psychologist,* 1–13.

History (2017). Columbine High School Shootings. Retrieved from www.history.com/topics/columbine-high-school-shootings.

Huesmann, L. R. (2007). The impact of electronic media violence: Scientific theory and research. *Journal of Adolescent Health, 41*(6), S6–S13.

James, S. D. (2009). Columbine shootings 10 years later: Students, teacher still haunted by post-traumatic stress. Retrieved from http://abcnews.go.com/Health/story?id=7300782&page=1#.Ua4zCuuXxTA.

Kato, P. M. (2010). Video games in health care: Closing the gap. *Review of General Psychology, 14*(2), 113–21.

Klebold, S. (2017). *A mother's reckoning: Living in the aftermath of tragedy.* London: WH Allen.

Koster, R. (2005). *A theory of fun for game design.* Scottsdale, AZ: Paraglyph Press.

Kowert, R. (2016). *A parent's guide to video games: The essential guide to understanding how video games impact your child's physical, social, and psychological well-being.* CreateSpace Independent.

Lenhart, A., Kahne, J., Middaugh, E., Rankin Macgill, A., Evans, C., & Vitak, J. (2008). *Teens, video games, and civics: Teens' gaming experiences are diverse and include significant social interaction and civic engagement.* Washington, DC: Pew Internet & American Life Project.

Markey, P. M., & Ferguson, C. J. (2017). *Moral combat: Why the war on video games is wrong.* Dallas, TX: BenBella Books.

Markey, P. M., & Markey, C. N. (2010). Vulnerability to violent video games: A review and integration of personality research. *Review of General Psychology, 14*(2), 82–91. doi:10.1037/a0019000.

Olson, C. K. (2010). Children's motivations for video game play in the context of normal development. *Review of General Psychology, 14,* 180–187.

Parents Television Council. (2011). PTC denounces Supreme Court ruling on CA video game law. Retrieved from www.parentstv.org/PTC/news/release/2011/0627a.asp.

Redd, W. H., Jacobsen, P. B., DieTrill, M., Dermatis, H., McEvoy, M., & Holland, J. C. (1987). Cognitive–attentional distraction in the control of conditioned nausea in pediatric cancer patients receiving chemotherapy. *Journal of Consulting and Clinical Psychology, 55,* 391–395.

Sestir, M.A., & Bartholow, B.D. (2010). Violent and nonviolent video games produce opposing effects on aggressive and prosocial outcomes. *Journal of Experimental Social Psychology, 46,* 934–942. doi:0.1016/j. jesp.2010.06.005.

Sheff, D. (1999). *Game over: Nintendo's battle to dominate an industry.* London: Hodder & Stoughton.

Squire, K., & Barab, S. A. (2004). *Replaying history: Learning world history through playing Civilization III.* Indiana University Bloomington. Retrieved from http://website.education.wisc.edu/kdsquire/REPLAYING%20HISTORY.doc

State of Connecticut (2013). Report of the state's attorney for the judicial district of Danbury on the shootings at Sandy Hook Elementary School and 36 Yogananda Street, Newtown, Connecticut on December 14th, 2012. Retrieved from www.ct.gov/csao/lib/csao/Sandy_Hook_Final_Report.pdf.

Teti, J. (2010). No Fun, Vol. 1. *Kill Screen, 1.*

Turkle, S. (1994). Constructions and reconstructions of self in virtual reality: Playing in the MUDs. *Mind, Culture, and Activity, 1*(3), 158–67.

Vasterling, J., Jenkins, R. A., Tope, D. M., & Burish, T. G. (1993). Cognitive distraction and relaxation training for the control of side effects due to cancer chemotherapy. *Journal of Behavioral Medicine, 16,* 65–79.

Archetypes
6

What Are Archetypes?

Archetypes are considered to be images with universal meanings attached to them (Stein, 1998). They are a widely used and beloved way of experiencing and discussing life, but also one of the most difficult ideas or motifs to conceptualize due to the less than tangible existence they represent. The conceptual idea of these psychologically abstract and literal interpretations of our lives is usually associated with Carl Jung (2014) or James Hillman (2004) as the creators and identifiers of these themes. Archetypes are everywhere, yet have to be conceptualized from a metaphorical, symbolic, and non-literal approach to be used in therapy and commonplace life.

The etymology of the word archetype may lend some clarity to its meaning: archetype stems from the Latin noun of *archetypum* which in actuality is a Latinization, rendering of a non-Latin word to Latin origin, of the Greek noun *archetupon* (Liddell et al., 1990). *Archetupon* is a combination of two smaller words: *arche* and *tupos* which merge creating the meaning: an original pattern or constellation which all other similar persons, places, objects, concepts, characters, moods, behaviors, ideologies, and many more are derived or modeled after. Therefore, archetypes are the beginning models of all constituted behaviors we observe.

What constitutes archetypes are the similarities in which they are presented; they create an analogous thematic form of what is common between multiple scenarios, ideas, behaviors, objects, and images. People viewing them have similar emotions, even when events in which they occur are different. Publicly, we find most archetypes in books, stories, fairytales, and myths (Hillman, 2006,;Jung, 2014). These examples are considered to be the primary beginning stage of archetypes, or the first places to find them in our cultures, across the world. For example, a snowflake is symbolic for winter or air conditioning, while a print of a sun means summer or heat. Similarly, blue is considered conceptually to mean cold, while red is the equivalent to hot. Place these pictures on anything and the person viewing them can understand the representation quite simply. Archetypes are even experienced by individuals across varying cultures and identities. This is what makes archetypes so powerful and exceptional to direct experience; they are commonly felt and experienced across Earth including through the play of video game avatars even though they are within a virtual space (Bean, 2015; Hillman, 2004; Jung, 2014). These patterns can be seen through historical texts, art, religion, fables, myths, and in the case of this book, video game characters. Only by viewing them from this point of reference does one begin to see the importance of how they are intertwined into everyday life, therapy, and psychology.

Epistemology of Archetypes

Psychology is deeply rooted in philosophy, similar to many current disciplines of critical thinking, so it is no surprise that the term archetype was first used by Plato with his archetypal hypothesis; however, he did not refer to them directly as archetypes, but as "ideal forms" (Stein, 1998; Young-Eisendrath & Dawson, 1997). How this is to be interpreted is to mean: our ideas which we have, our consciousness that we are aware of, and the abstract information which comes through our consciousness at any given time does not constitute ideal forms. This is because ideal forms are indeed aspects independent of consciousness or conscious thought; they exist independently of the object, thought, idea, or what another thinks of it. For example, the primary ideal form of beauty is ephemeral, everlasting, and requires the idea or concept of beauty to be thought of by a person in order to be brought into a conceptual existence therefore de-rendering the ideal form. The primary form of beauty is considered to be the most essential and purest experiential form of reality and truth. Regardless of whether an individual thinks about beauty, the primary and ideal form of beauty will always exist. However, once thought about, it loses the enlightened ideal form and becomes less abstract and more literal. After the *conceptualization* of beauty has occurred; beauty can be applied to different forms viewed in the environment creating an *entity* of beauty based upon the conceptual thought. In essence, an individual's random thoughts, enlightenments, and ideas are utterly and completely pure experience untarnished by outside influences and everyday involvement until

Figure 6.1 The Different Forms of Beauty

Artwork by Tara Packey, used with permission

they are impractically placed upon an object in the environment narrowing the ideal form to a single entity literalizing the concept.

Ideal forms do not comprise or include the materially or physically felt forms or objects through sensations of the five senses (also known as entities depicted in Figure 6.1), but are the original abstract existence of the form as depicted at the top of the picture. The thinking ideas create an arrangement of governing behaviors, cognitions, actions, and events felt, experienced, and expressed by an individual or seen by others surrounding the individual through their behaviors, words, and subtlety expressed nuances. These behaviors eventually become ingrained in our everyday life and grow into second-natured reactions. Put simply, we begin to prefer and place the idea of beauty upon self-preferred objects in our environment and after multiple completions of this cycle, it becomes unconscious. The reactions are exhibited in every situation we encounter, even if it is not appropriate for the surroundings individuals find themselves in. As we display these similar or identical behaviors consistently over a period of time; they develop into a pattern of sorts. This patterning of behavior is what psychology is interested in since the configurations can show a keen observer how an individual is more likely than not going to react in multiple areas of life. However, it is important to always attempt to bring the patterns back to the original and purest form. It is thought to be common knowledge that the best predictor of future behavior is past behavior, and this concept rings especially true when discussing archetypes and behavioral patterns.

These constellated behavioral patterns are what can be considered to be archetypes in a literal interpretation or format of existence. They are represented and seen through the different configurations of our behaviors, but require a careful and watchful eye to understand what the behaviors may represent. This is where the second part, and definitely the harder portion, comes into existence. An observer has to think about what the observed patterns represent, symbolize, and beckon us to understand an instinctual need of the person exhibiting them; almost reverse engineering the behavior back to the archetypal idea. Plato himself used his mentor Socrates's writings and theatrical plays to articulate these commonalities (Jung, 2014; Stein, 1998; Young-Eisendrath & Dawson, 1997). He discussed the characters being played throughout the various stories, their actions and behaviors, and highlighted the shared qualities and behavioral commonalities between them. These collective patterns were what Plato considered to be the ideal forms. He went on to even purport what Jung later additionally stated, that the ideal forms were universal and experienced by many people. This in turn is where many archetypes are seen in today's societies, through the writing and plays performed by actors portraying the archetypal energies of the character.

Jung and Archetypes

The "ideal forms theory" was later articulated and iterated upon further by Carl Jung (2014). Jung expanded this concept within the field of psychology to mean the idea of archetypes as psychological matter in our psyche rather than just ideal forms. What he meant by this was archetypes are psychological in nature and can only be found as originating within the mind and exhibited through our thoughts, words, and actions. Archetypes were, and are, past and present imaginal energies created and curated within an individual's presence and soul; personified through their behavioral patterns. Carl Jung believed archetypes to be images derived from the collective unconscious while being manifested metaphorically through Greek mythological writings (Feist & Feist, 2009; Hillman, 2004).

Jung's concept took the idea of archetypes further than just forms and constituted them as energies exhibited as thoughts and behavioral patterns. He advanced the idea of the archetypes by relating them to the human psyche. Jung also believed, as Plato did, we all experience these psychological archetypes from the collective unconscious or the consciousness of all humans. Archetypes were to be considered distinguishing configurations of behavior, thoughts, and ideas felt through an individual's unconscious or what is

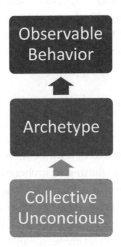

Figure 6.2 The Archetypal Path of Behavior

considered to be below the surface of our conscious or everyday awareness. These archetypes are thought to stem from the collective unconscious or consciousness of the world and its inhabitants; similar to Plato's "ideal forms." Archetypes instinctively come from the collective unconscious and are a basis of how we psychologically react, act, perceive, function, and behave as humans through our daily lives also known as observable behavior (see Figure 6.2).

I believe Robert Johnson best phrases the idea of archetypes appropriately:

> [T]he characteristics patterns that pre-exist in the collective psyche of the human race, that repeat themselves eternally in the psyches of individual human beings and determine the basic ways that we perceive and function as psychological beings.
>
> (pg. 27)

These configurations transcend historical texts, stories, art, religion, fables, and myths and can be seen as themes in dreams as well. Jung, as he continued to observe his clients' dreams and fantasies, became more aware of these parallels. Jung detected and began noting that the commonalities between his patient's dreams were symbolic representations within each of the client's dreams and imaginative states. Even though each client was different, they were having similar themes occur in their dreams. It is important to note that the clients Jung worked with had no interactions between them, had never met, were engaged in vastly different areas of society and employment, and were of different ages and gender. Physically, there were substantial differences in their everyday lives, but psychically, there were considerable metaphorical and thematic similarities. These representational and symbolic similarities later became known as archetypes.

Archetypes in Culture

These archetypal images are shared among people, found through our dreams and daily events, and analyzed to determine their important meaning. Many scholars have continued contributing to archetypes, such as Erik Goodwyn (2012) with his interpretation of archetypes, the gods, and neurobiology, Adolf Guggenbühl-Craig (2008) on the archetype of the invalid or psychopath, Veronica Goodchild (2001) with the archetypes of eros, chaos, and love, and Edward Edinger (1992) on ego and archetype to name a few. Today, with the addition of new and novel experiences, archetypes continue to be represented through a multitude of new experiences including movies, books, video games, and many other observed and played activities.

Due to the aforementioned likenesses and types of images imagined, archetypes additionally induce related feelings and constellations of behavior between the archetype and the person feeling it. Archetypes are even experienced by individuals across varying cultures and identities (Johnson, 1986; Jung, 2014; Stein, 1998). This is what makes archetypes so powerful and exceptional to absolute experience; they are commonly felt and experienced across the world. Individuals reading this book at the same time or at different moments in life, two different athletes winning the gold medal in completely different events, Mother Teresa passing from our world. All of these events are interconnected by the loss felt, excitement coursing through the body, enlightenment of the concept finally understood; the people experiencing these phenomena may have the same archetypal thought or image snap into their mind, yet be hundreds of miles away from one another. These would be brief examples of the power of the collective unconscious. A similar feeling of excitement or sadness running through their bodies and minds because of a concept they finally understand, a phrase that speaks to their experience and existence, a loss they feel so deeply, but never met the person who

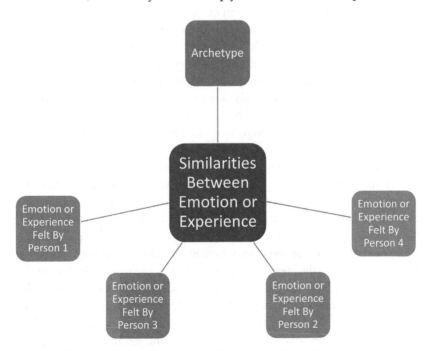

Figure 6.3 The Constellation of Emotions and Experiences into Archetypes

passed. How can this be? They would have to have a parallel feeling or idea forming at some point, however they never met yet understand what the other is feeling in their unique moment (see Figure 6.3).

A prime example of the collective unconscious's existence is when Princess Diana passed in August of 1997. The entire world mourned for her, but how many of us had actually met her? Why would we mourn someone we physically had no interaction with? Why did it feel as if we had lost someone we did not even know except through television, newspaper, and other forms of media? Jung would say the collective unconscious was being felt and experienced around the world through the death and mourning of Princess Diana.

We recognize these familiarities and cohesions in one another and relate these experiences to the character's experiences found in books, movies, myths, and video games to ourselves (Johnson, 1986; Jung, 2014; Stein, 1998). It is because we have had a similar experience; we can understand what others are going through emotionally, physically, and spiritually. Some may even call this singularity empathy, but miss out on the shared experience and interrelatedness one has with the phenomenon. Archetypes are found in a vast array of ideal forms and there are too many archetypes to conceivably list. Some of the media of expression of the archetypes and their nature can be found in totems, animal sightings or occurrences, myths, fairy tales, legends, and symbols. One has only to look and draw the connections.

These archetypes are found within everyday life and current culture. Individuals unconsciously identify with archetypes on a deeper and more personal level than what normally would occur. Most of the time, we are unaware about the resonation with the archetype(s) we are personifying, but sometimes others around us have an easier time viewing the persona being exhibited. These archetypes are neither good nor bad, but are justly present as a form of energy we, as people, feel, are energized, and directed by (Johnson, 1986; Jung, 2014; Stein, 1998). To place a distinction of good or bad would be a projection of our opinion upon the archetype(s). To be clear, archetypes can influence us in healthy and unhealthy, adaptive and maladaptive, functional and dysfunction manners, behaviors, and views compared to the world around us. These views may be considered to be socially dependent and derived. When the views are considered to be bad or socially deviant, an identification is placed upon the archetype narrowing the idea, literalizing the energy, and inherently destroying the experience itself through a negative viewpoint. However, when the archetype is seen as positive, society tends to swing to the other extreme, idealizing and idolizing the archetype to a point where it becomes unhealthy. In each of these cases, a polarization effect has occurred and disallowed the archetype to be seen for its own purpose or being, regardless of good or bad.

However, it is important to note while archetypes may sound beautiful and noble, they have both a light and dark, good and bad, or positive and negative side. To put this into an Eastern traditions perspective, every archetype has a yin and a yang, both are needed to be whole. We, as humans, strive to be in the light or positive side, but occasionally fall into the dark, or negative side. In order to find wholeness or completion, we must find the balance between both. This requires an acceptance of the darkness and a striving for the light. Without the acceptance of our dark side or shadow, we fall prey to it and tend to act out in our different environments usually spelling out disaster.

For example in one culture, an individual's behavior and values are comparably different from another culture's. A prime example is Japan's collectivistic culture versus America's individualistic culture. In Japan, one's individual rights, independence, and self-reliance are considered to be counter-cultural or shameful, whereas in American culture these qualities are highly valued. In each society and culture, different archetypes will be held to differing standards. Behaving in counter-culture ideals presents or highlights a negative view of one's behavior. A prime example of this is in a collectivistic culture online video games are held in high regard and played by millions of people. It literally has become part of their culture and a way for them to connect to one another. However, with some researchers from an individual-istic society it is deemed bad or addictive because of the time spent online and a perceived lack of social interaction. In these views what we forget is the difference between cultures is what makes us all unique. By pushing a standard upon them because of our viewpoint may be considered to be inappropriate and demeaning at best resulting in an archetype of power or a need of being correct; ironically narrowing our views and focus abilities. It is important to take care in our distinction of these archetypes and cultures as they are powerful instinctual energies and everyone has the possibility of experiencing them through different cultural interactions.

James Hillman (2004), father of Archetypal Psychology, states archetypes are "like psychic organs, congenitally given with the psyche itself," (pg. 14) believing everyone as having the ability to experience them, but in order to understand them on a deeper level; "one must turn to culture." Hillman additionally warns about the possibility of "literalizing" archetypes or making them "fixed." How this is interpreted is to mean reducing and trapping the archetype itself to meaning a literal object or image, thus not allowing it be expressed in different manners or metaphorically. Interpreting Hillman's suggestion of turning to the culture may indicate a need of understanding video game culture and video gamers through a different lens. One of the most common conceptualizations of an archetype—the hero's journey—demonstrates a constellation of an archetype most commonly found in books, video game stories, and personal experiences.

The Heroic Journey and Archetype

The composition of a hero is a complicated and treacherous path to undertake due to the trauma one usually must incur and the post-traumatic growth from the experienced trauma. A hero endures through a painful ordeal, usually in childhood, through psychological change directly resulting from the adverse experience. Heroes are not born, they are created (Campbell, 1972). After the post-traumatic growth a higher level of functioning occurs, after which the hero is unable to return to the state before. Batman is a prime example of this phenomenon due to his parents being killed by Joe Chill during his early years and forcing him then to rise from the ashes of his destroyed childhood, becoming Batman later on. Bruce Wayne cannot return to the state of his childhood even when he manages to find some solace in his actions later on—he is forever changed. Most video game characters have this phenomenon ingrained into their storyline making each video game a poignant example, vision, and playing of post-traumatic growth.

The Hero archetype is of someone that follows the following general ideas and principles of the hero, regardless of gender. This means irrespective of your gender, male or female, you can and will undertake the hero's journey in some form over your lifetime and even multiple times through varying circumstances.

In order to be considered a hero, one must display and exemplify the ideals of said hero. These generally consist of facing adversity, danger, and odds in which one normally would not expect to have a favorable outcome; of having the courage to continue the journey despite the high chance of failure. Self-sacrifice is generally another part of the hero's personification or character commonly ending with the demise of the hero. However, in return, the saving of a person, companions, or world justifies the hero's destruction. Typically in the beginning of the story the hero is considered to be weak, amounts to very little, and is described as childish or having a childlike essence. The journey of the hero forces the character, actor, or avatar to take up the life's challenge thrust upon them and cast away their childlike nature for a grown-up and more mature state of being. Through their journey they gain expertise, power, courage, and knowledge of themselves with which to overcome their adversity, use their power appropriately, and join the adult world. Without the appropriate journey and acquired wisdom, the hero chances becoming a villain while believing he is a hero and savior of whom he is realistically subjugating and tormenting. These types of heroes are considered commonly found within all areas of life, including our own personal mono-myth as suggested and generally accepted by Joseph Campbell (1972).

Examples of the Hero archetype can again be found throughout history and in several forms, with many authors drawing conclusions from stories across many cultures. To give credence to the Hero archetype and its similarities, three specific examples have been chosen. It must be notated that these examples do not literally constitute the Hero archetype, but exemplify it through the actions, difficulties overcome, power found within, guidance, and similar patterns found within each story. Harry Potter, King Arthur, and Katniss Everdeen all exemplify the "Hero" archetype.

Harry Potter is a well-known story among all age groups. It is about a British boy who is tragically orphaned by the death of his parents and mistreated by his aunt and uncle's family. In the beginning of the series he is forced to live in a cupboard under the stairs, wear handed down clothes which do not fit him, and is generally treated as equivalent to dirt. This persists for a number of years until he is mysteriously visited by a stranger who tells him he is an important wizard. In the wizarding world, Harry managed to destroy a dark and evil wizard as a baby. In fact, Harry destroyed the same wizard who murdered his parents; the evil wizard was amazingly powerful and Harry miraculously managed to destroy him as a baby. He is further told he is to begin schooling at a place called Hogwarts "beginning his hero's journey." As he attends the school, the dark wizard continues to hassle and attempt to kill him through various manners and deceptions. Harry continues to thwart him and stay triumphant even against extremely unfavorable odds with the help of his friends and the guidance of the headmaster. This eventually culminates into the dark wizard being reborn and having a final battle in which Harry is victorious. Throughout the books Harry faces the adversity and danger of his wizarding world, but continues his journey nevertheless. He even sacrifices himself in the end in order to protect those he loves, giving truth and respect to his heroic actions. His journey was thrust upon him even though he did not want it. When he finally embraced it, not just as hero, but as a savior as well, he grew into his destiny.

King Arthur is another, yet different, hero in Britain's history with many stories being told of his heroism. He was born a king's son and heir to a throne, but was raised in a secluded and non-royal place. A farm of some sorts in the country with no knowledge he was heir to the throne of England. He was treated as a commoner and a "nobody" for most of the beginnings of his life. He eventually became a squire to a knight and was at a faire one day and pulled a sacred and significant sword out of a stone in the center of the town when he needed it for his knight. The importance of this sword was whoever pulled it would be crowned king of England as the writing on the stone stated. Arthur became King of England with one swift action. As he was young he sought guidance from a wizard known as Merlin and he heroically brought the country of England together with distinguished knights at his famous historic round table. He had to face continual adversity during these times and prove to the people of England he was the hero they deserved. With guidance and support from his friends he led England inspirationally forward in his heroic quest.

Lastly, the Hero's Journey is not just for the boys, as exemplified by Katniss Everdeen of the Hunger Games book and movie series. She is depicted as a poor child from her district in which she selflessly saves her sister from a yearly picking of children by sacrificially volunteering herself instead. In this picking, one boy and girl are selected randomly as "tribute" to be gruesome contestants of "The Hunger Games" in which contenders are forced to kill one another in order to claim achieved victory for their home district. Katniss comes from nothing, a poor family with very little to eat and survive on. However, through her journey of the games, friends she meets, and companions she chooses, she unknowingly ignites and begins a rebellion. She becomes the face of the revolution and is thrust into it even against her will. She takes up the reigns and fights for the people of the land. She is guided by other people throughout the books and movies, but has to begin to believe in herself in order to achieve her position as heroine. She has to cast away her childlike innocence and stand up for what she believes in: freedom from tyranny.

Each of these stories brings to light explicit and important characteristics. The stories are substantially different, but they each hold specific similarities and a reliance on internal strength and resilience. All three heroes began with nothing, were considered weak, and come from nothing of importance. They each were set against great odds and had to overcome them in order to succeed. The heroes sacrificed themselves in order to accomplish their goals as well. Their destinies were not wanted and they attempted to run from them in the beginning of their stories, but eventually took up the heroic mantle in order to become something greater than themselves. King Arthur's tale is more difficult to view, but his sacrifice comprises his entire life bringing the great continent of Britain together while the other two heroes were more literal interpretations of sacrifice. Each hero, Katniss, King Arthur, and Harry Potter had to heed the hero's call and rise to the challenge in order to fulfill their destiny. Throughout their journeys, they gained knowledge, wisdom, expertise, and demonstrated the true markings of a hero. These traits, standards, and principles are what constitute the Hero archetype and with enough searching, we can find these in our own lives. There are plenty of other characters who hold similar commonalities such as Batman, Mulan from the Disney movie, and Martin Luther King Jr. Once you learn to identify archetypes like "the hero" you will begin to see examples of it everywhere.

Possibly at one point in your lifetime you have to stand up to a bully, take someone's side in an argument you are not sure of, save a complete stranger from a burning building, form your own opinion or theory of how the world works, or even write a book or academic article. These actions require heroic energy in order to complete them. This is because you have to put yourself and your experience into a form which will be critiqued by others as they may not share the same direct experience. However, if you have enough history or experience, there is a high chance of being able to relate at least a part of it to their experience in some format. Overall, it requires internal strength in order to overcome the odds against you.

Video Games and Archetypes

As a point of reflection, reading and learning about the Hero archetype or watching the story or myth of the hero around us through books, movies, and everyday life is eye-opening and important. However, video games bring a different perception and experience for the hero's story, as *the video gamer is able to direct and play as the hero*. This establishes a substantial motive of why individuals enjoy the video game realms so abundantly. While playing, they are instinctively being able to participate in the myth of the hero, not just watching, reading, or observing it. In this logic, the playing of the video game is an exceptionally important action for the player as they become part of the story. However, when the story is or begins to become stale or stagnant, we usually see a decline in the participant's play and enjoyment of it regardless of the medium.

A speculative look on a current video game example of this would be World of Warcraft. The Blizzard video game holds the record for the longest active and most subscribed to Massively Multiplayer Online Role-Playing Game (MMORPG) to date. At its prime, through storytelling and use of the hero's myth, the video game had 12 million subscribers at the end of 2010 (Brown, 2010). However, with the implementations and changes across the video game over the years, the number has substantially dropped to a still impressive 5.6 million video game players after quarter two in 2015 (Watts, 2015). Some video gamers believe it lost its core audience because they were trying to make it easier for everyone to play. Personally, as an active player throughout the years, I believe the game itself has lost its myth of being a hero in the virtual world. Not surprisingly, with each new expansion the subscription number increases dramatically for a period of time and then has a substantial decrease shortly after. Activision, Blizzard's parent company and maker of World of Warcraft, reported it was "expected and consistent with our experience following prior expansions." With each expansion and major content addition their fan base wonders if the game maker managed to re-find their hero myth again then leave the game because they are again disappointed. In summation, though archetypes are ephemerally eternal, if they do not grow or evolve then people can mature past them. When we lose the archetypal energies holding our curiosities, we lose the energy to stay fixed on one place, action, or video game. In retrospect, it is no wonder these actions occur and why retro video gaming has been increasing; because the Hero archetype is more easily found and associated with in these older mediums. It is encouraging in the fact we thrive on these experiences and the different worlds have the ability to give their experience to us. Without it, we may have to primarily rely on our own mono-myth which at times becomes stagnant.

What makes video games unique, compared to mythological archetypes, is their conceptualization of archetypes in a literalized visual format, rather than relying on the imagination and interpretation of the reader as in literature or a board game. Video games take archetypes even a step further than a visual medium like movies because the archetype becomes an interactive experience to be played. Video games literalize the archetype played by the video gamer choosing to interact as one of them. The video game character or avatar itself is a literalized representation of the archetype created by the video game developer. The image of the archetype, the avatar played, gives it life, but the playing of the character gives it meaning. What is meant by this is that the character is only a character comprised of pixels. Without the video gamer to interact, move, and have the character explore, it would not exist past the pixelated stage. By playing as the character, the video gamer brings meaning to the existence of the pixels. As a gamer, an individual brings life to it and provides meaning for the created virtual character. The storyline in which the avatar is played, whether chosen through a linear path or open world fantasy, is as important, if not more, to the image of the archetype. It helps us create a specific narrative for the character which may represent internal manifestations of our own personality. It further enhances our experiences and understanding of real world problems, solutions, and mannerisms in which to handle difficult situations we encounter.

Greg—A Case Study

To explore this concept further, a clinical example is exceptionally useful. A child named Greg came into my office in a constant state of mistrust in his current surroundings, including his family. Greg was socially isolating himself and withdrawing from his parents at home. Additional concerns were his traumatic background including physical and verbal abuse, his traumatic abuse difficulty with his biological mother, and complications with social isolation at times in many facets of life. For example, Greg had close friends at school, but would become anxious and worried when physical altercations occurred. An example had been when his friends began play fighting with him at school, Greg became anxious and wanted to leave the area and his friends out of a fearful reaction to the aggression his friends were demonstrating.

Greg had additionally been unable to trust anyone besides his step-mother and biological father because he had been "hurt too many times in the past," including by a previous therapist. His past therapist had been able to build rapport with him and earn his trust, but had lost it when the therapist sided with his biological mother on visitation rights. Greg had seen this as a major problem due to his past altercations with his mother and felt abandoned. As a result, Greg became angry and refused to talk to the therapist any longer. His parents worried about his condition as a consequence.

As a result of his past, Greg became curious and immersed within video game worlds, specifically Garry's Mod and the Borderlands trilogy. He would play them or discuss them as he got home from school, when he had any additional free time, or with his friends. He became obsessed with the aspect of playing his character and "being good." Greg's parents expressed a worry about the video game worlds he chose to play in, but were unsure about the consequences.

I knew I had to build a great amount of rapport very quickly with him. He had lost rapport with this previous counselor because he felt abandoned and that his previous counselor was not working in his best interest. He expressed that playing video games provided a cathartic experience for him and

I identified that it gave him helpful coping styles. His father was playing the video games with him and helping him process the emotional content found within each virtual game. Through exploration of motivations we were able to hone in on a specific game to which he attributed much of his coping mechanisms and ability to process information. He said he felt powerful and meaningful within the virtual realm of this game. This videogame was part of a trilogy of video games called the Borderlands series and he played the entire series.

Through the multiple games of the series Greg was able to identify the progression of the characters in the video games and place them in sequential order even though they did not come out in that order. In actuality, the games came out at different times and across different worlds, but Greg continually played the same character or avatar within the virtual videogame in all three of the playable scenarios or virtual realms. During our analysis of his characters played, Greg came to the realization that he was playing a heroic journey continued throughout all three of the different video games.

Through examination of Greg's conscious thoughts, choices within the videogame, and experiences outside of the videogame, we were able to identify and work on his own personal heroic journey. This occurred very quickly because of knowledge that I had of the videogame and I was able to relate it to his personal experience, including his trauma. Even with this personal knowledge of the video game, it was imperative I suggest themes and archetypal play that I, as the therapist, saw through his video gaming experience. The reason for this was because I may have seen different archetypes that may not have been present for Greg and thus would not have been true of his virtual and real life experiences. If I continued to force different archetypes or experiences upon him that did not synchronize with his view of himself, then they would not be meaningful or have any relevance to his experience. This would be an example of therapists forcing their ideals upon the client and not necessarily listening to the client's experience; this would have hurt our rapport, but also would have impeded our work in allowing his experience of the video game to unfold. The important matter at hand was to find the experience that created a deeper connection in order to properly understand and allow Greg to consciously identify with his character(s). As a result, after multiple analyzations of his game play, he felt as if he played the video games to understand his personal heroic journey. We discussed the heroic journey he had to go through in each of the video games and how he experienced them. In addition, there was another main character that was not playable, but was in all three virtual realms. His name was Handsome Jack.

We discussed Handsome Jack at length. Our first interpretation of Handsome Jack was an explanation of where he may have gone wrong in his thinking and greed. We were able to determine in the first videogame he was a hero working for the cause of good by helping out the players through the sales of in-game items and hints at where to explore next. In the second game, Greg was able to decipher that Handsome Jack had begun to change in his thoughts and patterns when talking to people (the players) and acting out through maladaptive behaviors and uncordial words. Finally in the third installment, Handsome Jack became the villain; you had to have a final showdown with him in order to beat the game.

Working together we were able to look at the timeline of the heroic journey of Greg himself, and Handsome Jack. We discussed the archetype of the hero, which Greg was playing, and the archetype of the villain, Handsome Jack, who was heroic in a different sense but much smaller-minded and had tunnel-vision. Upon further discussions and Greg's personal analyzations of the composition of a hero and a villain, we were able to determine that a villain was just a misguided hero in Greg's eyes. Overlapping this new distinction for Greg provided differential insight into his videogame play. Furthermore, we overlaid the general concepts found within the videogame to his actual life and trauma, discussing how he had found his own personal hero, and how his anger was Greg's own personal villain. Whenever he became angry and lost control, his villain-side was coming out because he could only see one thing, his anger and narrow-mindedness. However, his hero-side shined through much more often than his villain-side. Once he was able to understand when his villain part of his own personal hero myth was approaching within his cognitions, behaviors, and words, he was able to put a stop to it. He was able to begin to understand when his personal villain was approaching consciousness and was able to take a step back to control his maladaptive emotions. He understood why it was happening and was able to make a meaningful memory and knowledge from it all because he had the virtual experience to rely on from play the Borderlands Trilogy.

Greg was eventually able to see that his resilience lay in being a hero: having to overcome such a travesty, being able to push through it and continue on in life, and the knowledge that he has many supporters in his life enabled him to let go of most of the anger. (In truth, this is where most of his drive had come from over his life and will continue to come from for an extended period of time in his life.) Greg, having been set on his personal journey of understanding his own resilience and personal heroism, was then ready to leave the therapy room and begin to mold his myth of being his own personal hero. His video game play had been instrumental in his post traumatic growth from his previous trauma. His avatars and preferred play were an outlet for him to grow and feel empowered to continue forward with his life.

I was given an opportunity to hear about his updated progress a few months later. His parents reported that Greg appeared to be more outgoing, understanding of his emotions on a greater expanse and level, and that he was making new friends and allowing his experience to unfold naturally. His parents reported he used to "hold back" in conversations and "be unsure of himself." They reported being amazed at his transition in school, friendships, family life, and attributed it to the different interventions applied during our therapy sessions. Luckily, his parents were willing and constantly there to help him transition and understand the video game and its applications to his real life; this appears to have been transformational for Greg. Without their extended help it may have been a slower transition overall. His parents provided crucial interventions at home to help with the processing of his emotional and physical trauma through his playing of video games.

Video games have powerful and transformational archetypes embedded in them as playable characters. These manifestations are not solely found in virtual realms, but are born of the essences of their own manifestations. This is what makes video games, their characters, the storylines, and the back story of the game so transformational and enticing. The player is given the chance to wield magic, hunt in the woods from afar, get into the face of the enemy with their sword or axe and strike fear into their hearts. While fantasy can provide a different place to claim a unique lifestyle the video game allows you to experience it while still living life, anyone should jump at the chance to experience a rebirth. The playing of the game in itself is not detrimental, but an opportunity to begin anew or become more stout in one's resolve teaching the player different opportunistic abilities and rules to which we all live by, but have the regale of a story and hero behind it.

References

Bean, A. (2015, September). Dear Veronica: My video game addiction. Video Game Expert. Retrieved from: www.engadget.com/2015/09/23/dear-veronica-my-video-game-addiction/.

Brown, R. (2010). World of Warcraft subscriber base hits 12 million. Retrieved from www.cnet.com/news/world-of-warcraft-subscriber-base-hits-12-million/.

Campbell, J. (1972). *The hero with a thousand faces*. Princeton, N.J: Princeton University Press.

Edinger, E. F. (1992). *Ego & archetype: Individuation and the religous function of the psyche*. Boston, MA: Shambhala.

Feist, J., & Feist, G. J. (2009). *Theories of personality*. Boston, MA: McGraw Hill.

Goodchild, V. (2001). *Eros and chaos: The sacred mysteries and dark shadows of love*. Lake Worth, FL: Nicolas-Hays.

Goodwyn, E. D. (2012). *The neurobiology of the gods: How brain physiology shapes the recurrent imagery of myth and dreams*. Hove, UK: Routledge.

Guggenbühl-Craig, A. (2008). *The emptied soul: On the nature of the psychopath*. Thompson, CT: Spring.

Hillman, J. (2004). *Uniform edition: 1*. Thompson, CT: Spring.

Johnson, R. A. (1986). *Inner work: Using dreams and active imagination for personal growth*. San Francisco, CA: Harper & Row.

Jung, C. G. (2014). *The archetypes and the collective unconscious*. London: Routledge.

Liddell, H. G., Scott, R., Jones, H. S., McKenzie, R., & Perseus Digital Library. (1990). [*Liddell, Scott, and Jones Greek Lexicon* (Online)]. Medford, MA: Perseus Digital Library, Tufts University, Classics Dept.

Stein, M. (1998). *Jung's map of the soul: An introduction*. Chicago, IL: Open Court.

Watts, S. (2015). World of Warcraft subscriptions down to 5.6 million. Retrieved from www.ign.com/articles/2015/08/04/world-of-warcraft-subscriptions-down-to-56-million.

Young-Eisendrath, P., & Dawson, T. (1997). *The Cambridge companion to Jung*. Cambridge, UK: Cambridge University Press.

Video Game Archetypes 7

As archetypes are indeed present in video games and playable through virtual characterizations, it is important to hone in on and understand the different playable archetypal avatars. This allows the discussion to unfold about the character being played, what is intriguing about it, the game mechanics, powerful emotions and feelings, behaviors, personality, motivation, and the ability to use imaginative concepts putting forth psychological material crucial for therapeutic progress. Each video game, video game world, and created characters is unique to that specific world. A character cannot transfer to another world and be able to roam in a new virtual space. However, due to the similarities, components, and basic ideas found in each game, it is possible to discuss the characters as archetypal agents spread across each game; different in appearance, yet the same in constellation. In order to do so, it is imperative to discuss and understand the commonalities of different archetypal virtual characters.

Mythological stories hold the answer of understanding different archetypes and they are indeed too numerous to list them all, but in video games, there are not as many in which are experienced or played as. By the very nature of video games, video gamers are left with a much smaller archetype list to choose from and embody through their playing of the avatar. Additionally, due to the smaller list of archetypes, characters across different video games hold similar background histories and driving forces. Through examination of many video games ranging from 8-bit to AAA video games, archetypal commonalities begin to coalesce based on character qualities and circumstances. These characters can then be seen as existing across different video games in different avatar forms, but based in the same creational essence. While there is the possibility of many more archetypes being present in video games, currently I narrow it down to seven main archetypes of play, which transform the character into the archetype of the hero. However, there is another primary archetype which spurs development towards the hero archetype before becoming one of the seven main archetypes of play; the Orphan archetype can be found in all video game characters and their players.

The Orphan Archetype

Common culture portrays an orphan as a child or children who have lost their parents or been abandoned permanently (figuratively and literally) without the ability to care for them self or other siblings residing in a similar poor and/or poverty stricken environment (Bailey, 2009; Kurfi, 2011). As a result, the child or children feel abandoned, abused, and even neglected. Society's view of an orphan is no better if not worse. Society believes them to be under privileged and sometimes dregs of society, outcasts, or even scapegoats for when problems arise in a neighborhood or country. This results in poor prognosis for any child or adolescent labeled an orphan (Bailey, 2009; Kurfi, 2011). Overall, the impression given is that they are a waste of time and drain on humanity even though their predicament is not of their own doing. Examples are King Arthur, illegitimate son to the throne, Aragorn, a border ranger destined to be king in Middle Earth by Tolkien, or even Moses, left by the river by his own mother out of fear of him being put to death in Egypt. These stories present children with little to no support and usually are ostracized by other individuals forcing them to survive on their own.

Most common stories present the hero as an orphan because of the solidarity, humbleness, and tutelage such a history and involvement can provide. Only by experiencing and completing the journey through these difficult times and existential tensions can one truly become a hero—because they know what it means to suffer. Link in The Legend of Zelda video game is always an orphan at the beginning who has destiny thrust upon him in order to defend Hyrule and defeat the evil spirit which threatens the kingdom (Nintendo, 1986–2017). Throughout his challenges and the dungeons, he becomes more powerful, overcomes his shadow (even literally fighting it in some of the games), and has the ability to save the world from the darkness. Even though he started off as an orphan, detested and having no parents, he becomes a force to be reckoned with later in the game due to his humble

Figure 7.1 Orphan Archetype

Artwork by Joel Christiansen, used with permission

upbringing and perseverance. There is an inert power that the Orphan archetype has, an ability to overcome anything and appreciate everyone for who they are. Orphans showcase their strong ability to survive and be self-contained individuals striving for affection and attention from everyone.

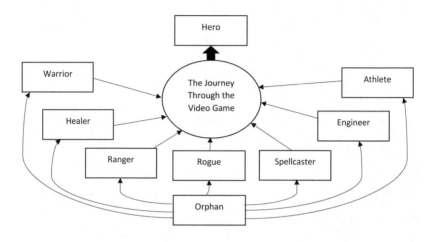

Figure 7.2 The Archetypal Journey Through Video Games

When playing as a video game character our internal orphan is "tapped" in order to have us grow closer to the character and storyline. If done correctly, a game has an undeniable pull towards completion which can be difficult to describe. Using the same The Legend of Zelda video game, Nintendo created a powerful myth around the videogame lore and personified it through the playing of Link. It activates the Orphan archetype in the player and has drawn millions of players into rapidly buying the video game once a new one becomes available. In fact, video game players usually have to wait every three to four years for a new Legend of Zelda title to be produced due to the intricate storyline and immersive experiences Nintendo puts into the game, which makes the draw even more powerful. The Legend of Zelda is not the only video game which taps into this potential of an orphan; almost every video game title does so in some form. The player has to work through the Orphan archetype in order to reach heroic greatness as depicted in Figure 7.2.

While the Hero archetype is the end goal and achieved through playing the character, there are other avatar constructions which the video gamer has to play through to reach the end point. The Orphan archetype is the beginning of the journey, but not the end even after reaching hero status. The seven main archetypes of play are the conduits through which a video game player reaches heroic greatness. Using Link in The Legend of Zelda as a further example, he begins as an orphan, but masters swordsmanship (Warrior archetype), magic (Spellcaster archetype), and ranged weapons (Ranger archetype) which leads to him becoming the hero at the end of his journey (Hero archetype), as shown in Figure 7.3. On occasion, as in The Legend of Zelda, there are multiple archetypes being played and all of them are the channels in order to reach the Heroic archetype.

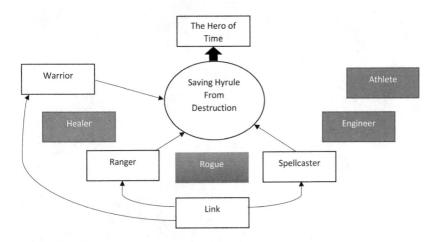

Figure 7.3 Link's Archetypal Journey

The Warrior Archetype

To exist, the warrior needs a battle to participate in and without it, the warrior would cease to be. Strength, vigor, stamina, broad shoulders, armor, muscular sinew on the body are generally what describes the warrior. Warrior energy is usually shunned due to the destructiveness of the Warrior archetype and it is also seen as careless and lacking in thought. However due to the impressive feats accomplished and abilities possessed, warriors are worthy comrades to have. If channeled properly, the warrior becomes a soldier who is resolved, has charisma, can be relied upon, and has nerves of steel (Campbell, 1972; Moore & Gillettte, 1990). In the movie Conan The Barbarian (1982), Arnold Schwarzenegger exemplified what a warrior is at his true potential, but before he was at the height of his existence, he was a barbarian fueled by

Figure 7.4 Warrior Archetype

Artwork by Joel Christiansen, used with permission

instinctual drives and careless acts. His journey made him a warrior and without it he would not have been able to reach his destiny. However, muscles and strength are not always what defines the warrior. For instance, Lara Croft is considered a warrior due to her cunning and impressive fighting skills, especially in one-on-one combat (Paramount, 2001). Prowess and critical thinking are also traits which need to be exhibited by the warrior spirit in order to rise out of barbarian ideology.

Video games portray the warriors as a "tank" of sorts, a person who can be in the middle of battle and endure a lot of pain and damage. In groups, warriors tend to be the leader of the group, jumping into battle, and keeping the focus on them instead of their comrades. They also can play as DPS which produces increased damage, but lowered survivability. Warriors tend to use brute and destructive force in video games to obtain their end goals, are prized for their fighting ability, but again do not rely solely on these means. For instance, in World of Warcraft (2017), a warrior is a melee character which runs into battle with two weapons or a weapon and a shield and causes massive destructive damage to a group or sole characters.

The World of Warcraft example above serves as one manner in which to envision the warrior, but in video games warriors come in many different forms which provides ample opportunity to play as one. Different avatar forms can be a knight, army soldier, marine, king, noble, prince, and many more. They can have different characteristics as well such as holy, earth, and even darkness attributes which aid them in their endeavors. Most times they are melee characters that focus on close encounters when fighting, because that is where they excel the most. With a warrior, keeping them at ranged combat usually proves to be life ending for them because of their need to be in close quarters.

When individuals play as a warrior in video games they tend to exhibit similar characteristics of the warrior in their real-life encounters. They are in fact caught by the Warrior archetype and use it to grind through their daily lives. For instance, a video gamer playing as a solider in Call of Duty or Battlefield tends to show aggressiveness and significant lacking in their tact ability when it comes to interpersonal relationships. Disagreements are common and are usually how conversations end. They enjoy the fighting aspect of the warrior, due to an enlightened "high" fighting and arguments can provide. Generally, their relationships are poor, superficial, and rely on aspects of bullying in order to get their way. This is the low side of warriors and requires a cautious eye in order to deflect their "attacks" and help them develop critical thinking in their motives and relationships. However, there are additional video gamers who have already moved past this beginning stage and begin using their archetype in order to be a shield for their friends and family, putting themselves at a point of risk. Using Conan as an example again, he was brute and hawkish in the beginning, but once he acquired guidance and began using critical thinking, he evolved into the higher end of the warrior and became a champion and devotional hero for his people. He was able to shield them from many dangers once he gained the wisdom and guidance he needed. Warriors require guidance and nurturing in order to hone their abilities and bring them to a higher side of critical thinking while becoming aware of their emotional power and how to use it appropriately.

The Healer Archetype

Life is full of surprises, trials, and hurt, creating wounds or injuries for everyone, whether physical or emotional. Healers spring from this need and have always been able to help heal these wounds, showing an aptitude for helping individuals process and move past the hurtful experiences (Hatcher, 2002). Healing is a journey that moves one through the initial challenge of the pain and torment from defragmentation of the spirit and body into a whole person. Shamans are thought to be the first healers the world has ever experienced (Merchant, 2012). They focused on healing the spirit of their patient through communication with animal spirits for guidance. Clearly this has evolved into today's practice of medicine, therapy, and doctors and while these professions may not use similar arcane practices, they have to give notice to their roots (Ellenberger, 2006).

The healer ensures that their friends stay healthy and inspires them to continue forward. They do not attempt to be the center of attention, but are more introvertive and reserved with their words which makes them appear humble and wise. Individuals who are healers can feel superior to others due to their ability to keep everyone harmonious. Healers tend to stay in the background and enjoy the company of others while supporting them emotionally and physically (Hatcher, 2002). The healer tends to stay focused on others rather than themselves, sometimes failing to care for their own needs. The amount of energy and devotion to others can be overbearing to them and unnoticed because of their more reserved qualities. They feel the need to help others at the detriment of their own selves.

Mythological stories and video games tend to portray healers as frailer individuals robed in cloth and carrying a spell book of healing incantations (Tarcher, 2002). Healers can be seen as anyone in a role which has qualities of a doctor whether they are in a war zone healing comrades or in a dungeon

Figure 7.5 Healer Archetype

Artwork by Joel Christiansen, used with permission

keeping allies alive. Generally, they use spells or healing tinctures to keep their buddies alive and well. They support the team overall from being wiped out, removing negative status effects, and buffing character's abilities. All games have a form of this character in the storyline—especially MMOs. They are considered to be essential in order to progress through the video game storyline or experience more difficult areas. Healers gain their power for spells through the use of mana and usually come from a specific line of healing magic. Whether it is holy, nature, spiritual, or even elemental forces, their spells are geared towards helping and healing.

Individuals playing as these characters tend to be more reserved, introvertive, and stay in the background of groups ensuring the survival of all players and friendships (Bean, 2015). They realize they are needed, but wait to be called upon in their moment of need. In real life experiences, healers tend to try to keep everyone harmonious and happy. Generally, they are seen as a good friend and ally to have in times of need. They do not rush into fights, but take a more cautious and optimistic approach to their lives. Individuals in this area usually are used and abused by others, but don't seem to mind in the moment because they feel they are being helpful. While this may seem as good and well, it drains the individual and causes distress in their life. Healers additionally tend to have low boundaries with others which is why they become drained so easily. They do not want to give up the positive feelings helping others produces and do not want to acknowledge they may be a part of their own distress. Healers require guidance to develop boundaries and appropriate helping of others to eliminate the detrimental aspect of losing themselves and being used for their helpful mannerisms.

The Ranger Archetype

The ranger is a versatile individual who relies on speed, agility, ranged combat, hardiness, cunning, and dexterity to finish off their opponents while usually being resistant to nature magic. Usually they have a beast or animal which travels and hunts with them, but it is not a requirement. These range in different utility from a horse for speedy travel to a wolf for unrelenting combat. The ranger focuses on their ranged weapons rather than spells or melee combat like bows, guns, mortars, throwing knives, and grenade launchers (Tweet & Collins, 2012; Tyler et al., 1976). Unlike the warrior, melee combat usually spells trouble for the ranger whereas staying at ranged combat decisively ensures victory. While melee combat is not their forte, they do have abilities which other archetypal classes do not get, such as dual

Figure 7.6 Ranger Archetype

Artwork by Joel Christiansen, used with permission

wielding swords or long knives, but their melee combat abilities pale in comparison to the warrior.

Rangers are the border riders living away from populated areas and finding solace in nature. They prefer to be alone and away from society as they believe it can be a perversion of natural reality. Rangers are scouts, pathfinders, bounty hunters, trackers, woodsmen, hunters, and beast masters (Tweet & Collins, 2012; Tyler et al., 1976). In their own environment, they are unbeatable due to their self-sufficiency, craftiness, and constant awareness of their surroundings. They are consistently adaptable to their environments and blend into the woods or wastes without a trace. While most rangers can be considered loners, some choose to help guide others through difficult terrain and safely through wilderness.

Combat is not usually worrisome for rangers due to their superb hunting skills and marksmanship. Usually in video games, the ranger has a sniper ability which allows them to cloak easily and efficiently pick off other players or NPCs in the video game. They have an intuition similar to a sixth sense when an event is about to occur and can easily predict their opponents moves and actions. Rangers tend to stay steps ahead of their prey and easily ensnare others into cleverly laid traps. Of most importance to the ranger is their ability to produce high damage to their quarry and then quickly fade back into the shadows of their environment. This makes the ranger a unique and powerful ally to have.

Aragorn from the Tolkien series is a prime example of a ranger (Tyler et al., 1976). He lived in the shadows of the outer rims of Rivendell protecting the borders from deathly creatures who would otherwise attack the town. He was bestowed with superb tracking abilities and cunningness which allowed him to stay hidden when he wished to be. Aragorn did not have a beast companion, but did exhibit animal magnetism in his role as a ranger. He ends up helping the Hobbits in their quest and eventually becomes the human king of the land beginning the new era. Aragorn was extremely adept with a multitude of weapon proficiencies which proved to be important throughout his life for his survival.

Video game players who choose to play as a ranger tend to be more introversive as they prefer ranged combat over the melee (Bean, 2015). These player's interpersonal lives tend to have a lower number of friends they would deem to be close. They prefer solitude and their time to themselves not fearing relationships, but avoiding them at times usually out of anxiety and fear of rejection. In conversational groups, they tend to stay on the outskirts and watch the group encounters interjecting at times which may be seen as random and sometimes explosive. They tend to stay hidden and "attack" out of the shadows for safety, quickly withdrawing if their interjection does not fair positively. They have strong boundaries and do not let their guard down often or to many people. Wariness is of second nature to them due to their strong peripheries and lowered interpersonal relationships. Rangers require a steady and calming hand to show them that being vulnerable and open to developing close interpersonal relationships does not have to be viewed as a possible negative outcome creating anxiety. They tend to believe not being close to another person or not obtaining appropriate social praise means they are not worthy.

The Rogue Archetype

Rogues are similar to assassins and spies and rely on surprise attacks, playing in the shadows, stealth capabilities, careful and cunning watching, and most of the time have an invisibility ability which makes them very difficult to see (Tweet & Collins, 2012). They can be seen as mercenaries who are willing to complete any job whether it is stealing, spying, killing, or vicious enforcement upon others. They rely on brutal and efficient melee tactics which have a large damage output and can incapacitate their target. Their dexterity and intelligence levels are what make them a most powerful individual to face in one on one combat (Tweet & Collins, 2012). Through keen observation of a situation, rogues tend to have a plan in order to get out alive amongst other plans to gain the most out of any situation. They can be considered a mix of the warrior with their powerful melee attacks and the ranger with their cunning and stealth capabilities. However, just like the ranger, if they cannot destroy or subdue their foe quickly, they are in trouble with melee tactics and usually need to retreat from the battle.

Weapons usually used by a rogue are daggers, fist weapons, traps, and one handed weapons which are usually dual-wielded meaning they can use two one handed items at the same time—one in each hand. The primary reasoning behind this is the rogue needs to be able to be light and nimble on their feet in order to complete their contracts. They also need to be able to make a quick escape if their life is threatened or they find themselves in a fight they cannot win or become overpowered. Rogues cannot survive on their own forever due to their lowered survivability when they are constantly on the run, do not have a break to rest, and therefore usually belong to a guild of some sort with other rogues. The guild typically has a strict code of conduct where no rogue is allowed to harm another individual unless it has been

Figure 7.7 Rogue Archetype

Artwork by Joel Christiansen, used with permission

contracted out to them. This prevents the guild from being targeted by authorities and having other rogues run rampant in the world.

An example of the rogue archetype is Boba Fett, a male bounty hunter set in the Star Wars movies (Century Fox Home, 2013; Wallace et al., 2016). He was cloned from the infamous Jango Fett, a master assassin and bounty hunter, but did not accelerate in his growth as normal clones did. Boba was raised by Jango's son and learned the master of assassinating and bounty hunting while growing up. He was later on labeled a bounty hunter, but Boba Fett can be considered a rogue due to his scoundrel like abilities. He even created a syndicate of bounty hunters taking on dangerous missions throughout the galaxy earning him the reputation of one of the deadliest bounty hunters and assassins. He used tactics, hiding in the shadows, cunning force, misdirection, and traps to ensnare his prey. He may be labeled a bounty hunter in the movies, but he has a rogue like archetypal essence.

Video gamers who play as a rogue as their primary character prefer the shadows and not being seen by others. They feel alienated by others and not part of the regular community at times. There may be an inherent fear of being seen or relating interpersonally to others. This usually is a first focus of the therapeutic encounter to determine what may be the cause of the fear. However, there are other reasons for preferably playing this archetype such as one does not like to be the center of attention, the gamer may be introverted, have some hostility issues, and prefer to have quick quips in groups causing a disturbance and then leaving the conversations in a stealthy manner. They usually see themselves as different from others and isolated while in larger groups. Focusing on the destructiveness of the actions, behaviors, and language of the rogue is a must. Unfriendliness towards others who do not appear to understand them usually is an emphasis as well in the therapy room.

The Spellcaster Archetype

From a druid who casts incantations to the most studious wizard who learned their craft in a library, the Spellcaster archetype is one which is quite powerful. There are many names which the spellcaster is known by: mage, wizard, sorcerer, witch, warlock, magi, sage, magician, and more (Tweet & Collins, 2012). As one can surmise from the name, the main abilities are casting spells. The spells can be healing, buffing, or damaging to players. Magic users such as the spellcaster come in many different forms and use a variety of magic. For instance, they can be earth, elements, fire, ice, shadow, dark, white, red, and even black. The type of magic used is usually indicative of the color and what elemental form it takes. Even so, sometime the color can signify the level of spells they can learn. As an example, in Final Fantasy, a white mage is one who focuses on buffs and healing spells while a black mage solely relies on harmful magics, and a red mage is a mixture of both yet master of neither. However, this is not the only manner in which spellcasters use magic—some summon demonic creatures to aid in their abilities as the warlock can in World of Warcraft.

Like other ranged characters, the spellcasters fight from a distance. This is because they are considered to be "glass cannons" with the ability to amass heavy firepower through their spells and long range, but are weak in close quarter combat. Spellcasters are individuals who study the different magics in order to become master of them all, although some will focus on specific schools only. They can usually be found in robes and using staffs or staves as their main weapons although on occasion they can be seen holding a spellbook or another off-hand item which grants them special bonuses and powers. Easily taken down if caught in melee range, they are still a formidable opponent. Spellcasters revel in the unbounded wonders of all magical entities and focus on expanding their knowledge of the known world while discovering hidden gems of knowledge.

Easy examples of well-known spellcastera would be Merlin from the Arthurian Legend and Gandalf from the Lord of the Rings (Lawrence-Mathers, 2014; Tyler et al., 1976). These two characters are well known for their magical prowess and also their intellect and knowledge—traits always found in spellcasters. As can be seen by video pictorials of these two wizards they use simple weapons, are not very proficient with any type of armor or shield, and focus on their spells. They both coveted and collected esoteric knowledge and were wary of whom they shared it with because, as with all spellcasters, knowledge is power. When they decided to share their knowledge with individuals, they were chosen carefully and appeared as wise old men while acting as mentors to their chosen individuals. While depictions of spellcasters are usually older men with white hair and long beards, this is not always the case.

Video gamers who chose to play as spellcasters believe they are on the outside of the community or general population feeling different than others, but hold a general wisdom to their lives. They may or may not fear closer interpersonal interactions in large groups, but also find a place to mentor others in various domains in which they are proficient. Interpersonal relationships can come easy to them, but they are wary of them as getting close to another individual means you have to connect in a different fashion

Figure 7.8 Spellcaster Archetype

Artwork by Joel Christiansen, used with permission

than just acquaintances. As a result, spellcasters tend to be introverted, but open to social aspects of life. They are usually proud individuals who have some difficulties in parts of their lives which require some guidance and understanding of their history. With a predisposition to knowledge seeking, spellcasters tend to seek out knowledge and understanding of their lives and are open to different and unique ideas. Allowing them to gain knowledge from the therapist in the room is a key feature and needed in order to progress therapeutically.

The Engineer Archetype

Steady, calculating, patient, and methodical—this is what the Engineer archetype represents (McGonagle & Vella, 1996). There is not a puzzle that will not be solved, a challenge overlooked, or an achievement not attempted. The task itself becomes an engrossing endeavor with special care being administered within the game in order to fulfill a specific goal. Stability is a key attribute that is found when one plays as the engineer. A significant reason is due to the massive amount of focus and planning which one has to conceive in order to mitigate the negative aspects of planning (i.e. unhappy populations due to crowding) versus increasing the positive outcomes (i.e. growth and more in-game revenue).

However, creativity is another attribute which is important for the engineer player. They create their destiny in the video game world from building skyscrapers to amusement parks, to entire civilizations. These endeavors require significant amounts of creativity in order to achieve the goals, and tactfully avoiding confrontations which would be costly and knowing the correct time to strike. The engineer is an inventive problem solver who uses creativity to come up with logical and practical solutions (McGonagle & Vella, 1996). If they do not succeed the first time, they continually change their approach until they have been able to manage the puzzle or NPC in front of them.

It is important to not take the idea of the engineer into a literal inter-pretation of a video gamer who tinkers with machinery to defeat individuals. Indeed this is a pigeon-holed mentality of thinking. The engineer is also a tactician of grand scale war combat. They marshal troops to battle attacking hordes. They research technologies at appropriate times to combat their enemies and gain footholds on distant worlds. The battlefield requires a tactical mindset in order to overcome the odds. This is the true nature of

Figure 7.9 Engineer Archetype

Artwork by Joel Christiansen, used with permission

the engineer, no matter what the problem is or the odds against them, the player is able to complete their destiny by engineering a victory. In essence, they engineer their own destiny in video games starting from the beginning.

Video gamers who play as an engineer are tactful in their interactions with others. They have a need to express their creativity in multiple forms or face a feeling or inferiority. The ability to manage their own destiny in the video game world can be extrapolated to the real world to show the ability of engineering their own personal destiny. The darker side of this archetype is due to the constant calculating aspect of an engineer while battling for superiority. It has a mannerism of having the video gamer take logic to the extreme and disregarding human emotions. Most CEOs have this difficulty when building and running a business. They do not take into consideration the difficulties their decisions will have upon their employees. While their calculations may seem like they have chosen the correct path, reality sets in and shows the individual that it believes otherwise. This leaves the engineer questioning how everything went wrong. Emotional content of decisions are a focus of most therapy sessions. It is important to make decisions with not just logical and rational choices involved, but additionally how will it affect others emotionally.

The Athlete Archetype

At first thought one may be left with the image of an Olympic hero on a podium acquiring their gold medal for winning 1st in their game or activity when thinking about the Athlete archetype (Amidon, 2012). This is just one aspect of the athlete. The Athlete archetype is one which includes many different forms of competitive video game play. The main attribute that comprises this archetype is the competitive spirit of the video game player. They enjoy the competition and thrive in it, but also understand the pleasures of just playing the game. The athlete is always available for a challenge or playing with another individual to determine who is superior.

In fact, society has begun to see more of this type of play with the inclusion of E-Sports (electronically facilitated competitive game play). Many different teams have sprung up playing StarCraft, League of Legends, and even Hearthstone to name just a few. These events draw hundreds of thousands of viewers and even more hopefuls of being able to play upon the big stage or a packed arena with thousands in the adoring crowd. The organized competitions award large sums of prize monies, salaries, and sponsors to the

Figure 7.10 Athlete Archetype

Artwork by Joel Christiansen, used with permission

players. This form of playing the video game has become such a large part of video game culture that developers have even begun to build in these competitive aspects of video gaming into their games.

The athlete explores their capabilities and relies on their quick actions, keybinding (the practice of assigning various abilities upon the keyboard allowing an individual to hit one key to complete multiple commands), and reflexes within the virtual world in order to overcome the odds against them. They participate in the competitions in order to determine the winner, but sometimes do not know their limits either. This is one of the darker sides of the athlete. They tend to push themselves to their extreme to find their limits. However, they have a difficult time acknowledging that they may have found their personal bounds. The athlete tends to always be on the go and always trying to push their personal boundaries, not just in the video game, but also in their real life. They require a guiding hand to determine what is considered to be too much and how to handle different circumstances. The athlete enjoys the power of the game, but has a hard time with acknowledging their limits. Personal drive is usually not an issue as the player is always attempting to fine tune themselves, but they do require the breaks to rest and rethink.

The Villain Archetype

Evil villains intrigue everyone. This is because villains complete acts of horror which we believe we personally could never commit, even if pushed to the edge of having to make a decision of living or committing an atrocity against another. The act of hurting another individual purposely attacks our psyche in a manner causing disgust and stress. The villain is the extreme evil-doer and does not feel this same sense of guilt or regret. Villains attack and subjugate other individuals without a reason or in order to conquer everyone and take control the world. They share a contempt for society as it stands, believing it to be wasteful or requiring subjugation to bring about a more idealized order (Cowden, 2011). Every video game has a villain in it, whether it be a boss at the end of dungeon or raid, an end-game bad guy, or failing to achieve a goal in time (with the player being both the hero and the villain). They are the main target in which the player's goal is to level up, obtain new and unique powers, and defeat the evil threatening the world or society.

The villain is the polar opposite of the hero, morally and figuratively. The hero must stand up and face the villain in the video game. In essence, it is the hero's shadow and the hero is the villain's shadow (Cowden, 2011). They require one another to exist, have to face off to determine who is superior,

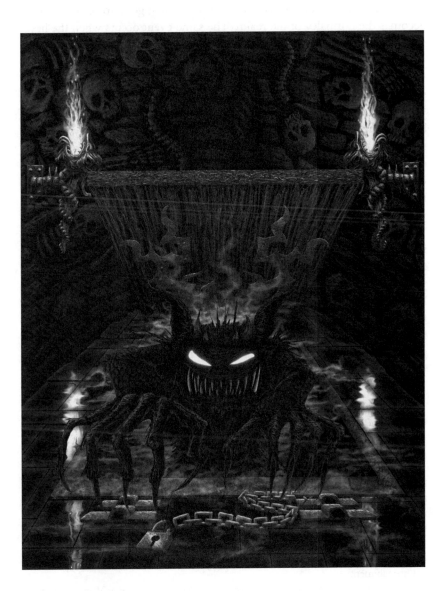

Figure 7.11 Villain Archetype
Artwork by Joel Christiansen, used with permission

but cannot live without one another. If the hero falls and the villain wins, there is no evil any longer because there is nothing good to oppose it, evil becomes the normalcy of the realm. The same event occurs when the hero wins out.

An important distinction one has to make is that in order to defeat a villain, one must think like one at times. Villains are fallen heroes who have succumbed to their ego rather than staying focused on helping others. It is true of the proverb "one dies a hero or lives long enough to see themselves become the villain." If a hero lives long enough, they eventually begin to think they know what is best for everyone. They have saved them on multiple occasions, right? Why wouldn't they be the one to know what is best for everyone else? This is the dark side of the hero—if the player succumbs to the ego thinking that they are the only savior people have, they usually slip into the villain role.

The player's main goal in almost any game is to defeat the villain. If one is not apparent, we make our perceived opponent into one in order to justify attacking or beating them. It is a common tactic to succeed in the virtual world. We have to feel we have a reason in order to justify our actions. However, if the player falls into the villain role, they must be worked with to explore their possibly maladaptive thinking, at times believing they are fighting a villain outside of the virtual world as well. This requires careful guidance, providing clarity and tranquility to the player to prevent falling victim to the villain role.

References

Amidon, S. (2012). *Something like the gods: A cultural history of the athlete from Achilles to LeBron*. New York: Rodale.

Bailey, J. D. (2009). Orphan care: An introduction. *Social Work & Society*, 1.

Bean, A. (2015). Video gamers' personas: A five factor study exploring personality elements of the video gamer. Retrieved from ProQuest Digital Dissertations. (AAT 3726481).

Campbell, J. (1972). *The hero with a thousand faces*. Princeton, N.J: Princeton University Press.

Century Fox Home (2013). Star Wars: I, II, III. Beverly Hills, CA: 20th Century Fox Home Entertainment.

Cowden, T. D. (2011). *Fallen heroes: Sixteen master villain archetypes*. Las Vegas, N.V.: Few Cow Productions.

Ellenberger, H. F. (2006). *The discovery of the unconscious: The history and evolution of dynamic psychiatry*. New York: Basic Books.

Hatcher, M. (2002). *The healer archetype fieldbook: Practices and resources for personal and professional leadership*. Flagstaff, AZ: Creative Communications.

Kurfi, M. H. (2011). *Societal responses to the state of orphans and vulnerable children (OVC) in Kano Metropolis, Nigeria*. Saarbru_cken, Germany: LAP Lambert Publications.

Lawrence-Mathers, A. (2014). *True history of Merlin the Magician*. New Haven, CT: Yale University Press.

McGonagle, J. J., & Vella, C. M. (1996). *A new archetype for competitive intelligence*. Westport, CT: Quorum Books.

Merchant, J. (2012). *Shamans and analysts: New insights on the wounded healer*. Hove, UK: Routledge.

Moore, R. L., & Gillette, D. (1990). *King, warrior, magician, lover: Rediscovering the archetypes of the mature masculine*. San Francisco, CA: HarperCollins.

Nintendo. (1986). The Legend of Zelda. [video game]. Kyoto, Japan: Nintendo.

Nintendo. (1987). Zelda II: The Adventure [video game]. Kyoto, Japan: Nintendo.

Nintendo. (1992). The Legend of Zelda: A Link to the Past [video game]. Kyoto, Japan: Nintendo.

Nintendo. (1998). The Legend of Zelda: Ocarina of Time [video game]. Kyoto, Japan: Nintendo.

Nintendo. (2000). The Legend of Zelda: Majora's Mask [video game]. Kyoto, Japan: Nintendo.

Nintendo. (2003). The Legend of Zelda: The Wind Waker [video game]. Kyoto, Japan: Nintendo.

Nintendo. (2006). The Legend of Zelda: Twilight Princess [video game]. Kyoto, Japan: Nintendo.

Nintendo. (2011). The Legend of Zelda: Skyward Sword [video game]. Kyoto, Japan: Nintendo.

Nintendo. (2017). The Legend of Zelda: Breath of the Wild [video game]. Kyoto, Japan: Nintendo.

Paramount. (2001). Tomb Raider. Hollywood, CA: Paramount.

Tarcher, J. P. (2002). *Healer: Transforming the inner and outer wounds*. New York: Putnam.

Tweet, J., & Collins, A. (2012). *Dungeons & dragons: Player's handbook, core rulebook I, v.3.5*. Renton, WA: Wizards of the Coast.

Tyler, J. E. A., Tolkien, J. R. R., Tyler, S. A., Reilly, K., & Zucker, J. (1976). *The Tolkien companion*. New York: St. Martin's Press.

Universal City Studios. (1982). Conan the Barbarian. Universal City, CA: MCA.

Wallace, D., Windham, R., Fry, J., Brooks, A., Corroney, J., McHaley, M., & Grossblatt, B. (2016). *The bounty hunter code: From the files of Boba Fett*. Online: Amazon/47North.

The Importance of Play and Imagination

8

The steps feel slippery as you walk up to the final chamber, your hands glistening with sweat and cramped with fatigue. It is a good thing you have those special boots from the previous room to help you keep your footing, you appraise. The door looms in front of you. You shiver, anticipating what is behind the ornate door, dark, made of steel, and carved with vicious looking creatures. You have never made it this far in this dungeon and you only imagine what type of monster awaits you. You hear a low growl that shakes you to your core, but you don't have the time to be afraid, so you snap your attention back to the final task at hand. Your comrades wait behind you, anxious for the door to open and reveal the horrors within. The lights go out; the world becomes pitch black. You hear the creaking door as it opens and see nothing but a pair of red eyes peer at you from within the room. The growl becomes louder and lower, presumably hungry for the bones and flesh of your group, as you step slowly into the room, awaiting your fate by the final boss . . .

Reading this passage may elicit your imagination of what could be behind the door. A predator in the form of a dog? Maybe a mechanical beast of some kind? Perhaps a hydra with multiple mouths full of sharp fangs waiting to crunch down on the corpses of players who dare enter its chamber. Regardless of what monster awaits the group, the danger one senses likely haunts and creates anticipation for the person playing. It may make the group or individual anxious and scared to think about what waits behind the doors. However, it is common to fear the unknown and our imagination can easily conjure up our darkest fears. These fears can control our next actions, whether we choose to avoid the monster, or step up to the undertaking.

Video games can be used to work with the gamer to "step-up" in different circumstances of life. The game itself provides the example which can be utilized in any aspect of life. A person sees something that elicits fear (e.g. a job interview, a social party, interpersonal tasks, etc.) and either doesn't know how to face it and avoids it, or steps in front of it to confront the fear. The video game worlds provide these same examples time and time again. Figuring out how to metaphorically use these examples is the key point in this trajectory.

Fantasy and Make-Believe

Pretend play is a loosely structured form of play which includes role playing, creativity, and non-literal behaviors to increase the excitement and fun of the play. Taking on new roles is not for the sake of survival or necessarily a means to an end, but focuses upon the play and creative aspect of the imagination. Fantasy play and make-believe play is an important facet for children growing up, creating a safe place or setting in which to express their fears and desires (Lillard, Pinkham, & Smith, 2011; Taylor, 1999). By participating in pretend play or role playing, individuals are incorporating past experiences, knowledge, and integration of the world around them to conceptually understand what it means to be alive and cognizant. Previous research on play and make-believe demonstrates individuals who have better fantasy and imaginative abilities show better social competence, cognitive capabilities, and empathetic attunement to others (Lillard, 1993; Taylor, 1999; Weisberg, 2013; 2015). These qualities additionally are exceptionally useful for adults to use in different environments and facets of life later on, suggesting that having a strong fantasy play ability in youth is important for future psychosocial development and living capabilities.

Although it can be tempting to dismiss fantasy play as "only a childhood activity," it is important to realize the cognitive and psychosocial benefits throughout the human lifespan. More specifically, pretend play has been theorized and shown to shape cognitive structures such as symbolic understanding, theory of mind, and counterfactual reasoning (Bateson, 1972; Weisberg, 2013; 2015). Briefly stated, the earliest form of play is described as object substitution in which the child uses an object (i.e. a bottle) for a purpose outside of its original intent (e.g. a rocketship). Pretend play then transforms later on through the use of invisible objects (lacking in physicality) and further on the concept of enactment play where the child dresses up in a form of role play (e.g. dressing up like a parent and cooking in a small scale replica of a kitchen) (Bourchier & Davis, 2002; Bretherton, 1989; Lillard, 1993; Weisberg,

2015). The distinction between reality and pretend occurs during this latter portion of development.

A major concern for parents is whether aggressive play, whether pretend or not, will turn their children into aggressive and violent individuals. There is no basis for this claim, as all children across cultures develop a form of play using aggressive means (Gleason, 2013; Jones, 2003; Weisberg, 2015). In fact, repressing the act of play and imagination can have a detrimental effect on the cognitions, behaviors, and emotional outcome of children. It invariably stunts their ability to differentiate between reality and fantasy and merges the two concepts into a dangerous point of reality. Children's transcendent function will effectively be repressed and their striving for wholeness at their developmental level will not be fulfilled. By having the ability to safely play with violent and aggressive concepts this inhibiting is much less likely to occur and children will use these experiences to continue developing their cognitions and mental abilities (Gleason, 2013; Jones, 2003).

Fantasy play has an additional benefit for anyone using it, especially children growing up: symbolic understanding. Symbolic understanding in play is the concept that children use objects, ideas, and actions to represent the other in their environment (Friedman, 2013). This can look as simple as the bottle used as a rocketship, picking up a banana and using it as a telephone, or pretending a stick is a sword. As Weisberg (2015) states "In pretend play, behaviors do not have their typical effects in reality, and objects may not have their typical properties" (pg. 251) which allows the imagination to grow and bear important fruits of mental capabilities. This is considered to be a form of theory of mind or the ability to mentally represent the other and understand needs, desires, and beliefs. Piaget (2015) and Vygotsky (1977) both believed that symbolic play was a crucial factor in children's development of social and cognitive abilities. By utilizing symbolic play in childhood and on into adulthood, an individual's theory of mind is continually being developed and explored. The play itself is considered to be mentalistic—understanding the mental states involved (Friedman & Leslie, 2007; Weisberg, 2015). There is knowledge that the object has a reality form and use and in the moment has a fantasy form.

Children generally do not mistakenly confuse pretend play and reality and can distinguish between fantasy and actuality by an early age (3–4 years, see Weisberg, 2015). For instance, Weisberg (2015) points out that "children in the banana-as-telephone game do not end up with mistaken beliefs either about bananas' communicative abilities or the edibility of telephones" (pg. 251) due to the aptitude of differentiation. As such, children are much more aptly aware of their surroundings and the distinction between fantasy and reality. While this may be a concern for parents who observe their children turning everyday objects into swords or guns, it can be considered a normal facet of life and should be allowed to occur. When parents are worried about concepts they observe, a good unwritten rule is to participate in play with their children to further enhance the developmental concepts, but more importantly be available for discussions surrounding reality and fantasy.

Playing Around

Play has been a conceptual need throughout the lifetime of man. The concept has been used throughout different societies as a primary and necessary condition of exploring and understanding culture. At the essence of cultural play, Johan Huizinga (2016) believed that culture itself was play and that different cultures have different rules of play. These rules of play dictated the culture and were not created by the culture, but are the culture. Further down the historical perspective psychologists such as Melanie Klein, William James, Sigmund Freud, Carl Jung, and many more came to the conclusion that play is only confined to the human species, but Huizinga believed that play is used in all forms of life. Dolphins play with one another in the water, monkeys have created their own games, and insects have even been observed participating in rituals similar to humans playing. Huizinga further reported in his seminal book *Homo Ludens* (2016) that play has always existed, presupposes human society, and that every life form participates in a form of play because of the aspects of fun play can have.

Huizinga (2016) identifies five characteristics that play must have in order to be considered play:

1. Play is free and is in fact freedom.
2. Play is not ordinary or real life.
3. Play is distinct from ordinary life both to the locality and duration of the play.
4. Play creates order and is order. Play demands absolute and supreme order.
5. Play is connected with no material interest and no profit can be gained from it.

Huizinga takes the concept of play even further by believing play is a cultural phenomenon which should be studied for a full understanding of the concepts and organizing play structure. Play can be expressed as an apparent language and in itself is a language which is begging to be understood by observing the play in its initial form through the conclusion of it. It serves a function to play with others and to utilize the imagination of the players creating a different structure outside of the normal human realm of societal existence.

Suspending belief and normal life has a cauterizing effect on difficult situations which arise from general reality. Children use these forms of play in order to process their emotional content and later understand an underlying meaning to the difficulties of life. When a child is expressing violence in a form of play in the therapy room, it does not necessarily mean the child is a violent sociopath, but that they are processing an event which they experienced, requiring the clinician to carefully glean an understanding from the symbolic play. The play serves as a way to process the emotional content in a natural manner and within a safe place, helping to reduce the tension psychically felt by the child.

Roger Caillois (2001) later built upon the theories of Huizinga, adding more comprehensive forms of play and criticizing Huizinga's focus upon the competition of play, believing instead that play can be more than just competition. However, he similarly places the concept of play into six core characteristics:

1. It is free and not obligatory.
2. Is it separate from the routine of life and occupies its own time and space.
3. It is uncertain as the results cannot be pre-determined and player's initiative is involved.
4. It is unproductive as in it creates no wealth and ends as it begins.
5. It is governed by rules that suspend ordinary and routine laws of behavior that must be followed by players.
6. It involves make-believe confirming existence of imagined realities.

Caillois argues that the complexity of play and games can be understood through four elements of play. The four forms of play can be combined in various manners to produce different games, but are also on a play continuum from *ludus* (structured activities with defined rules) to *paidia* (unstructured and spontaneous) depending on the form of play. Rules make the game more defined and increase the competition while reducing the chance factor, role playing ability, and perception alterations. Moving towards the *paidia* side of play, competition lessens while chance, role playing, and altering perceptions increase.

- Agon—Competition (e.g. chess, football, the Olympics)
- Alea—Chance (e.g. coin flipping, dice, slot machines)
- Mimicry—Role playing (e.g. cops and robbers, astronauts, costume play)
- Ilinx—Altering perception (e.g. spinning on a merry-go-round, substances, virtual reality)

Video games provide these same principles as outlined as play by these theorists. To play video games is to play a game which has established rules of what can be done and what cannot. There are more than normal physical pieces in this case, such as the digital environment and characters which have a three dimensional shape to them on a screen. However, even with these variations, the concept of play continues to be apparent.

Using the same six principles laid out by Caillois (2001) video games and the act of playing them can be seen as the defined logic of play. They are considered a form of free play, whether played alone or with another, and are not obligatory, they are separate from the routines of daily life and occupies a virtual dimension outside of our current immediate environment; the result of playing video games is uncertain of winning or losing, there is no creation of wealth from the act of playing excluding virtual coin within the game, which is considered to be not equal to physical monies, each video game has their own set of rules which must be followed in order to progress forward and complete the game, and by playing there is a confirmed existence of imagined realities of the game played.

Furthermore, evaluation of the four elements suggests that video game play is a form of play. Video games are comprised of many different aspects of virtual worlds, each ripe with its own constituents, rules, regulations, and linear pathways. There are aspects of competition, chance, role-playing, and different yet vital perceptions found in all video games. A player usually competes with the computer within the video game to complete a task or save an idea, person, or land, albeit there is usually player versus player interactions built into the game as well. There is a chance for better and higher gear from different bosses and quests, but also the chance to gain nothing, or a poorer version of the gear a character needs; individuals can role-play within their characters, changing their appearance, clothes, and identity within the game, but additionally through the use of costume play at conventions and in real life interactions, while different perceptions of the world can be seen through the graphics, storyline, and perceptions of the characters created within the video game.

An interesting point further illustrating the complexity of video games and the concept of play is on occasion a video game will have another game built into the virtual world. An example of this was in the recent addition to the Blizzard Franchise of Starcraft II: Wings of Liberty (2010). While in a portion of the game, between missions, the player has an opportunity to move around their home base of operations and interact with their characters, occasionally unlocking new and unique dialogues. Within different rooms there were objects with which to interact, one of which is a video game arcade machine where the player was able to play a version of a computer game within the game. The player was able to control the game as if they were actually playing the game itself, indubitably playing two games at the same time. This entices the player playing as the virtual character to play another game inside of the game, creating a metacognitive form of play.

Indeed, the act of playing video games is in fact play and therefore should be examined from a theoretical perspective of play itself. Video games and video gamers are and have a culture of their own, requiring the use of a phenomenological point of view to understand the ethos. This type of ethnographical approach can be used within any setting, but is most powerful when used in a therapeutic atmosphere with a skilled clinician. Understanding the draw of each world and the player's reaction to playing within it helps to provide knowledge upon the psychological draw of a different culture defined by the rules and regulations of the different avatar worlds, the composition of the gamer's avatar, and initiative shown through the programming of the storyline.

It is important to note that even though when discussing the concepts of imagination, play, and make believe, most scholars and clinicians may only believe the concepts to be important to children. This is not the case. In fact, most adults play and use their imagination on a daily basis, with friends, and even in recreational activities. For instance, playing board games utilizes the imagination and can stimulate the fantasy and play of any individual playing. Board games have become a way for adults to participate in an activity with friends and families. Another instance of adult play is costume play. This is where individuals dress up as a fantasy character and even act as them. They are usually seen at "Cons" or conventions surrounding a specific topic such as comic books, art, and video games. Common Cons which people may be familiar with would be the PAXs (South, West, and East) and San Diego Comic Con. They are considered to be the largest ones, but there are many others such as Wizard World, which travels around the United States, and New York Comic Con. Additional examples of adult play are murder mystery dinners, escape rooms, Medieval Times, and even theme parks. Clearly, play is widely used in everyday life and for more than just children.

The Power Within

Monsters of the mind are an everyday occurrence for anybody. That fear of what could happen or how to solve a problem which looms ahead of the person is difficult to describe because logically, one does not know where that dread of the problem ahead of them comes from. The difficulty can be anything: an additional work load placed on a person and whether he will have the time to finish it, a child's first haircut, the first day of a new school, whether she will be able to go outside of the house today, whether a relationship with another individual will lead to happiness or sadness, moving out of a comfort zone, or even of what the future holds. The aforementioned concerns are called "fear of the unknown." When an inability to predict the future comes along it creates an anxious response based out of fear.

Describing this fear can be very difficult because it is nothing more than a personal, mental obstacle. Every time an unfamiliar encounter occurs the manifestation of the fear begins again. This difficulty also creates a natural fight, flight, or freeze response to the situation. The response chosen will depend completely on previous situations experienced and how they were resolved. If the situation is similar to one previously experienced, the preceding experience will be helpful in curtailing the current predicament, and the person will fight against the fear. If the fear is too overwhelming it causes the state of freeze and the person will do nothing out of the fear. Lastly, there is the flight aspect which is when a person will run away from the situation leaving it unresolved.

Humans have always been afraid of the unknown because there is no certainty in it. Nevertheless we continue forward in life anyways. The human spirit is full of the courage to trying new things in the different facets of life, but it sometimes takes more than just courage to tackle a new situation. The ability to anticipate the consequences of a particular event is of extreme importance to anyone. Is it why not knowing what will happen can be so scary, we don't know what to expect when we land back on our feet at the conclusion. This fear is innate to everyone when they are experiencing a new and novel experience therefore it is unsurprising that there is a stigma for the unknown.

The fear of the unknown is common to the virtual worlds of video games as well. In fact, some video games like Five Nights at Freddy's prey on the fear of the player in order to make decisions to stay alive at night from homicidal animatronics. The opening portion of this chapter is a depiction of what one may experience while playing video games—a fear of what is awaiting them in the next room and whether they will be able to conquer it or fall to their demise.

With the myriad of video games available for purchase, opportunities to fight this fear of the unknown abounds. A key characteristic of the fear is that one does not know what to expect. Video games give the player the opportunity to face the fear based on their own personal power. Their characters develop throughout the game and grow more powerful as the player continues through the story. The story of the character showcases great feats and abilities which a normal individual in the real world likely does not have, but can experience through the video game and their character. Furthermore, the video game allows the player to try multiple times to defeat the bosses; at first, the player may be locked into place by the fear, or run from it, but eventually be able to overcome it by repeated attempts suggesting an overcoming of the fear and a place of resilience.

The story of their character is what makes the fear lessen because the video gamer has developed the character. The player learns the weaknesses of the enemy and then exploits them with their acquired skills—similar to how one learns coping skills for difficult and different life events. Once an enemy's weakness is known, it is no longer scary. It can no longer hold the same power over the person and instead becomes a known instance with a method in which to deal with it. What is more interesting and important is that the player is able to use their character to deal with the fear as they have been combating hardships throughout the game. Through the relationship with the avatar the fear has been conquered through the combined power of the player *and* the character. By overcoming the fear in the video game, the video gamer has learned a method in which to appropriately appraise a situation and then use tools and experience at their disposal to overcome a difficult situation. This same method of defeating a boss in a video game can be extrapolated and translated to real life encounters of similar proportions.

What Video Games Offer

When video games first came into existence and were becoming more mainstream and plentiful there was a push in research to determine whether they were helpful or a hindrance. Early research into the phenomenon of video games suggested that electronic play led to low motivation, social interactions, and could lead to obesity. More recently, researchers have seen more benefits of play and less disadvantages of electronic play for mainstream video game players. For instance, online video games and gamers have shown less anxiety in social situations, less depressive symptoms after playing, have been helpful for positive self-esteem, social interactions, and with certain clinical disorders such as Autism for safe and social engagement (Adachi & Willoughby, 2013; Durkin, 2010; Durkin & Barber, 2002; Ringland, Wolf, Faucett, Dombrowski, & Hayes, 2016; Shute, Ventura, & Ke, 2015; Valkenburg, & Peter 2011).

Historically speaking, play has been able to provide positive outcomes for personal and social development in youth. Previous research has shown that adolescents become more motivated and engaged in activities during and after participating in forms of play. Further benefits have been increased self-esteem, problem solving, richer interpersonal interactions, lowered anxiety and depressive symptoms, higher academics, and more positive social benefits and psychological well-being. Physical development has additionally been positively linked to play when the play involves a form of physical exertion such as sports.

Due to societal beliefs that video games create murderers, aggressive individuals, and other stereotypes created through moral panic (as discussed in Chapter 5) video gaming did not have the best chance of success as a medium of entertainment at first. Luckily research has been able to move society past much of the literal interpretation that playing a game will cause you to act exactly like the character played. This is an unfounded correlation as explicated through the aforementioned benefits listed above; Jones (2003) cautions about literalistic thinking and mentality due to the overlooking of important characteristics found within media mediums. It reduces the ability for an observer to pick up on the emotional content of stories and images.

Every story, image, and game has an emotional content which on occasion requires some sifting through to find it—but it exists nevertheless. The emotions may be difficult to understand for some not experienced with them (i.e. rage, empathy, happiness) or not even be seen due to a misconception of the storyline or misinterpreting a scene (i.e. crying due to happiness). Exploring these emotions in a safe and controlled context is a crucial part of experiencing and understanding life. When one feels rage, they are angry, as if they have to act, as if someone made a personal attack upon them, and they feel threatened. Happiness is on the opposite side of rage, a mental or emotional state of well-being described as positive contentment to flourishing joy. How does one know what these states of being are without feeling them? Stories embrace these emotions and show them through facial features, images, actions, and behaviors. Stories dive into the heart of these emotions and difficult states of being, portraying them efficiently and expertly, without whittling down and losing the experience.

Video games have stories which can elicit these same emotions. The exception is that the player is usually playing within the game therefore experiencing it as the character as well. The emotional content is usually portrayed throughout the storyline and images shown upon the screen. It is even projected upon the player as they experience it in real time. A qualifying event of this was in Final Fantasy VII (1997) when Aerith Gainsborough (translated into English: Aeris), a beloved character having exceptional healing potential, is killed in the middle of a quest as part of the storyline by Sephiroth. Most players when first experiencing this are astonished because it is completely unexpected. Cloud Strife is devastated by the loss, eventually completing his psychological break with reality, while Sephiroth is unmoved by the killing blow (Murray, 1997).

Playing video games has the ability to help conquer our own fears by defeating the monsters within the video games. When first entering a boss or minion fight the music changes to more rapid and higher pitched tones, exciting the player and causing them to focus on the game further. The beginning of each altercation can be a bit of a scary situation because one does not know what to expect. All of the senses are constantly feeding information to the player as he or she is attempting to figure out how to defeat the boss. The boss looms ahead and causes a sense of fear—a fear of the unknown of what will happen or how to defeat this conundrum ahead of the player.

The relationship, and the defeating of the fear concepts, can be extrapolated from the video game into real life using the same variables the player used to develop their character to appropriately handle their difficulties. With the experience of defeating a monster it creates an opportunity to use the same processes in which to handle life experiences. The video gamer had to complete specific tasks to obtain victory and therefore this manner can be used in real life as well. The power comes from the time spent playing, the storyline, and how the video game player handles the difficulties. The character's experiences can be a base to start from and conceptually understand what the problem is (i.e. the boss) while utilizing the power of the avatar to solve the difficulty.

Using these concepts in this manner changes the psychological dynamic of the problem being experienced. It helps remove the personal mental obstacle originally created by the video gamer. Utilizing the character's power and trying different tactics to defeat the boss is a form of problem solving and it takes the player out of a state of freeze and flight while putting them into a positive place of fight or courage to handle the situation. Furthermore, any previous example of real life encounters, including virtual happenstances, similar to a real life problem can be further used to help the situation unfold by looking at the parallels between the video game difficulty and the real life one eventually finding a solution.

For instance, if a video gamer is worried about attending a social event because of emotional anxiety he can become immobilized by the fear and freeze. However, if the video gamer has familiarity with this or a similar experience, maybe by joining a guild and introducing himself to others as an avatar in a virtual world, it will dissipate the original fear. This is due to the previous experience the video game gave the player in a social context. This example can be a starting point to work to change the entire experience for the player in other situations. Therefore, the video gamer already has the tools to work toward a place where the fear is no longer in control; he knows how to defeat it. He has experienced the fear of not feeling accepted, but attempted, regardless, to complete the task, likely due to lesser feelings of insecurity, both in the game and in his real-life scenario of the intimidating social event. This strategy can be quite phenomenal when used appropriately. This is just one of the important experiences and tools video games give to the player which can be extrapolated into real life experiences. The video game itself is a teaching tool for coping, development, and social skills in and out of the virtual world.

References

Adachi, P. J. C., & Willoughby, T. (2013). More than just fun and games: The longitudinal relationships between strategic video games, self-reported problem solving skills, and academic grades. *Journal of Youth and Adolescence, 42*(7), 1041–1052.

Bateson, G. (1972). *A theory of play and fantasy: Steps to an ecology of mind.* Chicago, IL: University of Chicago Press.

Blizzard Entertainment (2010). Starcraft: Wings of liberty. Irvine, CA: Blizzard Entertainment.

Bretherton, I. (1989). Pretense: the form and function of make-believe play. *Developmental Review, 9,* 383–401.

Bourchier A., & Davis A. (2002) Children's understanding of the pretence–reality distinction: a review of current theory and evidence. *Developmental Science, 5,* 397–413.

Caillois, R. (2001). *Man, play and games.* Urbana, IL: University of Illinois Press.

Durkin, K. (2010). Videogames and young people with developmental disorders. *Review Of General Psychology, 14*(2), 122–140. doi:10.1037/a0019438

Durkin, K., & Barber, B. (2002). Not so doomed: Computer game play and positive adolescent development. *Journal of Applied Developmental Psychology, 23*(4), 373–392.

Friedman, O. (2013). How do children represent pretend play? In M. Taylor (Ed.), *The Oxford handbook of the development of imagination* (pg. 186–195). New York: Oxford University Press.

Friedman, O. & Leslie, A. M. (2007). The conceptual underpinnings of pretense: pretending is not "behaving-as-if." *Cognition, 105,* 103–124.

Gleason, T. (2013). Imaginary relationships. In M. Taylor (Ed.), *The Oxford handbook of the development of imagination* (pg. 251–271). New York: Oxford University Press.

Huizinga, J. (2016). *Homo ludens: A study of the play-element in culture.* Tacoma, WA: Angelico Press.

Jones, G. (2003). *Killing monsters: Our children's need for fantasy, heroism, and make-believe violence.* New York: BasicBooks.

Lillard, A. S. (1993). Pretend Play Skills and the Child's Theory of Mind. *Child Development, 64*(2), 348–371.

Lillard A. S., Pinkham A.M., & Smith E. (2011). Pretend play and cognitive development. In U. Goswami (Ed.), *Handbook of childhood cognitive development* (pg. 285–311) 2nd ed. London: Blackwell.

Murray, R. (1997). *Final fantasy VII.* Bournemouth, UK: Paragon.

Piaget, J. (2015). *Psychology of intelligence.* Abingdon, UK: Routledge.

Ringland K. E, Wolf C. T, Faucett H., Dombrowski, L., & Hayes, G. (2016) "Will I always be not social?": Re-Conceptualizing sociality in the context of a minecraft community for autism. *Proceedings of ACM CHI Conference on Human Factors in Computing Systems.* 1256–1269.

Shute, V. J., Ventura, M., & Ke, F. (2015). The power of play: The effects of Portal 2 and Lumosity on cognitive and noncognitive skills. *Computers & Education, 80*(4), 58–67.

Square Enix (1997). Final Fantasy VII.

Taylor, M. (1999) *Imaginary companions and the children who create them.* New York: Oxford University Press.

Valkenburg, P. M., & Peter, J. (2011). Online communication among adolescents: An integrated model of its attraction, opportunities, and risks. *Journal of Adolescent Health, 48*(2), 121–127.

Vygotsky, L. S. (1977). *Opinion and speech.* Belgrade: Nolit

Weisberg, D. S. (2013). Distinguishing imagination from reality. In M. Taylor (Ed.), *The Oxford handbook of the development of imagination* (pg. 75–93). New York: Oxford University Press.

Weisberg, D. S. (2015). Pretend play. Wiley Interdisciplinary Reviews. *Cognitive Science, 6, 3.*

Understanding Video Gaming as Immersive　　**9**

The concept of video game addiction has become a worldwide phenomenon (Duggan, 2015). Nations like Japan and China have seen an increase in video game players enjoying more and more time online. Different countries have begun to research video game addiction as a problem that they observe in their countries (Bean et al, 2017; van Rooij & Prause, 2014). The concept of playing video games has become so rampant in the news media that it has spurred parental groups and some researchers to propose the link of video gaming to problematic behavior, violence, social isolation, and academic dysfunction (Gentile, 2009; Griffiths, 1991; 2000; 2008; Petry et al., 2014). Conversely, research has been able to show that most video game players do not experience substantial difficulties balancing their different environmental roles and playing their favorite virtual games (Przybylski, Weinstein, & Murayama, 2017). Of course, this does not induce the idea that all video gamers are not having difficulties—just not to the extreme that many portray it. However, even with a continuous, massive amount of research pouring into the academic field, there is still much unknown about the concept of video game addiction.

For instance, it is not called video game addiction, but Internet Gaming Disorder (IGD) within the DSM-5 and is labeled as a "condition for further study" (APA, 2013) Similarly, the International Compendium for Diseases Eleventh Edition (ICD-11) reference manual published by the World Health Organization has it currently as a category listed as "Gaming Disorder" with a focus upon impulsive and recurring gaming behavior (WHO, 2016a; 2016b).

Regardless, there are still many within the clinical field who have significant concerns with the current conceptualization of a gaming addiction, with even Division 46 of the APA putting out a policy statement about the concerns of this problematic diagnosis creating miscommunication across the psychological field (APA, 2018).Examining the criteria from both the DSM-5 and the ICD-11 sheds some light upon the area of apprehension and why scholars alike are hesitant to approve the notion of video game addiction.

To be clear, mainly researchers are the voice of opinion, dissenting or not, on this matter with very few clinicians tackling the subject itself. This creates a disparity between the research and the actual implementation of the research by clinicians. This gap between research and clinical implementation is not a new development, it has always been present and is one of the main reasons either side rarely dabbles in the other's area—mainly because they can't (Kazdin, 2008; Teachman et al., 2013). It is difficult for a researcher who only knows how to conduct studies and collect data to speak to the ability of working therapeutically with a patient when they have no training in it. It is possible to discuss it, but implementation is another level where many researchers are not experts. The same goes for clinicians. Most clinical mental health professionals are unable to work within the realm of research due to the demands of clinical work and lack of knowledge or expertise within the area. Clinicians can work with clients therapeutically and help out in areas of need, but being able to research is usually out of their abilities. Naturally the gap between the two disciplines of the same field continues to grow.

Many of the individuals who write the manuals that clinicians use for therapy, are distinguished researchers or office positioned individuals and it is unknown whether they have clinical experience working with individuals in a therapeutic setting. This brings about a concern whether the advisory groups for clinical classification systems know how to implement findings or the clinical validity of working therapeutically with individuals in times of need. The disparity listed above grows further apart due to this conundrum and lack of clarity and transparency.

Indeed this has occurred within the field of video game addiction; however, it then becomes the incentive and job for individuals who practice clinical psychology and have knowledge of the research of this area of the field to attempt to bridge that gap (Kazdin, 2008; Teachman et al., 2013). In order to bridge these two areas of clinical practice and research of video game addiction it is important to have the basic knowledge about the DSM-5 and ICD-11's attempt at creating a nosology of gaming addiction before discussing the theoretical underpinnings, or lack thereof, of the disorder itself.

Internet Gaming Disorder: The APA's Definition

Internet gaming Disorder (IGD) continues to be considered a "condition for further study," as it is currently labeled within the latest edition of the DSM-5 (APA, 2013). The American Psychiatric Association (APA) is encouraging further research into this area in order to provide further diagnostic clarification. As it currently stands the DSM-5 has rooted IGD's criteria analogous to chemical addictions and behavioral addictions, with adolescent males being reported as having the greatest risk of developing the condition. The DSM-5 additionally refers to IGD as synonymous with "Internet Use Disorder, Internet Addiction, or Gaming Addiction" (APA, 2013, pg. 796). Albeit there are numerous controversies about the boundaries of the diagnostic category (Aarseth et al., 2016; Bean et al., 2017; Griffiths et al., 2016; King & Delfabbro, 2014; van Rooij, van Looy, & Billieux, 2016).

Evaluating the risk and prognostic factors of the DSM's IGD category raises the concern about a larger and more prominent rise of the disorder in countries of "Asian descent", but not within Europe and Northern America as stated by the DSM-5 (APA, 2013, pg. 797). Functional consequences are reported to be school failure, job loss, and/or marriage collapse. Furthermore, the DSM-5 reports IGD to be compulsive in nature and "tends to crowd out normal social, scholastic, and family activities" (APA, 2013, pg. 797). IGD is reported to be a "pattern of excessive and prolonged Internet gaming that results in a cluster of cognitive and behavioral symptoms including progressive loss of control over gaming, tolerance, and withdrawal symptoms" (APA, 2013, pg. 796). However, no clear personality types have been established as a criteria for the disorder at this time.

The proposed criteria for IGD is the recurrent use of the internet to engage in games, as indicated by at least five of the following within a 12-month period: preoccupation with playing video games in individual's spare time; there are withdrawal symptoms when gaming is taken away or when the individual has not played for a period of time; there is an increased need to spend more time playing the video games; there have been unsuccessful attempts at quitting or stopping the playing of video games; there has been a loss of interest in other previously pleasurable activities due to video games; there is a continued use of video games or the playing of video games even with the knowledge that it is leading to difficulties across environments; the individual has lied to others within their environment about their time spent playing video games; the individual uses video games as a means to regulate their mood; and/or the individual has lost or had the potential to lose their employment, schooling, or other attained opportunity due to playing video games.

Gaming Disorder: The World Health Organization's (WHO) Definition

As of the current ICD-10 classification system, there is little mention of video game addiction, but as the latest ICD-11 is undergoing completion, there is a new category for Video Game Addiction called "Gaming Disorder." The classification of this disorder is the first of its type to be implemented within the clinical atmosphere of video games and addiction. The content of the new disorder had an open comment period where clinicians and researchers alike were allowed to comment upon the proposed content. This commenting period garnered many varying remarks about the lack of clarity of the diagnosis and the concern about implementing a disorder category without understanding the ethos of the disorder first (Kardefelt-Winther, 2016). Overall, the majority of the commenters agreed with the deletion of the proposed category, citing poor research and methodologies, a lack of clarity upon the topic, the suggestion that the proposed category may be more harmful than good, and a lack of evidence for the disorder. However, the Topic Advisory Group for Mental Health (Mental Health TAG) continued on with the creation of the disorder regardless.

Mental Health TAG created the following definition of the disorder "Gaming Disorder," with the addition of the following narrower classification terms: Digital Gaming Disorder, Internet Gaming Disorder, and Video Gaming Disorder.

> Gaming disorder is characterized by the inability to resist an intense internal drive to engage in gaming behavior ('digital gaming' or 'video-gaming'), which may be online (i.e., over the internet) or offline, manifested by:
>
> 1) Impaired control over gaming (e.g., onset, frequency, intensity, duration, termination, context);
> 2) Increasing priority given to gaming to the extent that gaming takes precedence over other interests and daily activities; and
> 3) Continuation or escalation of gaming despite the occurrence of negative consequences.
>
> The behavior pattern is of sufficient severity to result in significant impairment in personal, family, social, educational, occupational or

other important areas of functioning. The pattern of gaming behavior may be continuous or episodic and recurrent. The gaming behavior and other features are normally evident over a period of at least 12 months in order for a diagnosis to be assigned, although the required duration may be shortened if all diagnostic requirements are met and symptoms are severe.

(Mental Health TAG, 2017)

The Importance of Clinical Diagnoses

It is no surprise or secret that clinicians worldwide utilize both the DSM, primarily in the United States, and the ICD classification systems to identify and treat differentiating disorders. Providing a clinical diagnosis for individuals suffering from a cluster of mental health difficulties helps with identifying similar characteristics of the phenomenon and developing efficacious treatment plans which can be beneficial to the client. Knowing the variables helps guide treatment formulation, best practices, and interventions. A diagnosis can also provide validation for an individual who cannot mentalize what is happening to them, while giving them a guiding step towards treatment goals and clarification of their life difficulties. However, it is also important to note that the diagnoses which are routinely used in clinical practice have been thoroughly and etiologically researched over a multitude of years with significant and well-developed clinical studies to help with the formulation-not in the case of video game addiction (Aarseth et al, 2016; Bean et al., 2017; Carbonell, 2017; Krossbaken et al., 2017; Kuss et al, 2016; Quandt, 2017; van Rooij & Kardefelt-Winter, 2017).

The current state of video game addiction research is contentious at best within the research and clinical communities. In order for an appropriate diagnosis to be created, the criteria must be agreed upon (Aarseth et al, 2016; Bean et al., 2017; Carbonell, 2017; Krossbaken et al., 2017; Kuss et al, 2016; Quandt, 2017; van Rooij & Kardefelt-Winter, 2017). This has not been the case for video game addiction. The levels of severity, cutoff points, and rating scales are not in a consensus state of being at this time. This leads to the possibility of false diagnoses of video gamers who may meet some form of criteria for the proposed gaming disorder, but also have a healthy balance of other facets of life. The current state of our rating system utilizing the nosology of DSM-5 criteria based upon substance disorders does not take into consideration other aspects of video gamer's lives. Overall, it appears that a diagnosis is being formed upon a weak base of scientific data which is likely to cause more harm than help video gamers.

Research and Therapeutic Concerns of Gaming Disorder

As stated above, many researchers and clinicians have concerns about the addition of video game addiction. Indeed it should raise apprehension from a careful, critical, and watchful clinician. Many research papers have been published due to the trepidations raised throughout the field. While problematic gaming does deserve attention, the lack of clarity upon the subject and empirical basis for such a disorder has significant fundamental issues. In 2016, a group of 24 researchers and clinicians submitted a paper to the WHO topic advisory group, Mental Health TAG, suggesting significant concerns about the content of Gaming Disorder as proposed by the ICD-11. The concerns centered upon the use of low quality research to operationally define and monitor the proposed topic, the operational definition of Gaming Disorder relied too heavily upon substance use and gambling criteria, and a lack of consensus on symptomology and assessment of problematic gaming (Aarseth et al., 2016).

Further articles citing similar claims have been published raising concerns about the conceptualization of Gaming Disorder and the prematurity of the diagnosis (Aarseth et al., 2016; Bean et al., 2017; Griffiths et al., 2016). Conversely, other researchers have claimed there is a consensus of the disorder by means of a psychometric test to assess for the disorder utilizing DSM-5's criteria (Petry et al., 2014), but was quickly refuted by other researchers and clinicians who stated that the Petry et al.'s (2014) paper "does not provide a true and representative international community of researchers in this area" and "the published papers by the authors of the 'consensus' paper relied heavily on survey sample data, and completely omitted the core issues of clinical assessment and treatment-seeking patients" (Griffiths et al., 2016, pg. 167), further raising concerns about the validity of the diagnosis. Much of the research surrounding clinical applications suffers from clinical validation, fundamental psychometric issues, a lack of norm scores, information on measurement specific, standardized assessment, longitudinal case follow-up, distinguishability between high engagement and addiction, and can be considered to be atheoretical as it is based on faulty criteria not sufficiently indicative of distress or environmental impairment (Bean et al., 2017; Charlton, 2002; Charlton & Danforth, 2007; King et al., 2013; Przybylski et al., 2017; van Rooij, Schoenmakers, & de Mheen, 2017; van Rooij, van Looy, & Billieux, 2016).

An example of this is examined by Bean et al. (2017):

One area where there is lack of clarity regarding whether video game addiction represents a unique diagnostic entity or, in the cases of some individuals, is symptomatic of an underlying mental condition. To use one example, hypersomnia (excessive sleeping) is one symptom of a major depressive episode. However, we would not diagnose depressed individuals with hypersomnia with a comorbid "bed addiction." Further, individuals who read every day, throughout the day, are not considered to have "book addiction," although some parties may be more accepting of this type of "addiction" due to the social appropriateness of reading. Even more, watching American football and participating in fantasy leagues is not considered to be addictive behavior unless monetarial betting is involved.

(pg 4)

It begs the question of whether video game addiction is a societal push for a diagnosis rather than an understanding of the underlying characteristics. When social appropriateness becomes a driving factor of the diagnosis, concerns should be warranted about the suitability of the diagnosis.

Further evidence of Gaming Addiction being offered as a politically and socially presented diagnosis comes from the WHO themselves. In an email communication with one of the co-chairs and another member of the Mental Health TAG group it was acknowledged that there were political pressures regarding the creation of the Gaming Addiction category (personal communications occurring with Dr. Vladimir Poznyak and Dr. Geoffrey Reed; August–September 2016). The Mental Health TAG group and its members received "enormous pressure" from their "stakeholders to take into the consideration of the health aspects of excessive gaming," but also acknowledged that their "accumulated evidence reflected in the literature" was "indeed, not without controversies" and that "[I]ndeed there is no consensus among scholars on all aspects of "gaming" or "internet use" disorders, but it may never be achieved as in many other areas of public health" (personal communications occurring with Dr. Vladimir Poznyak and Dr. Geoffrey Reed; August–September 2016). This should not be deemed as the WHO creating diagnosis without regard to scientific discovery, but that there are significant societal and political pressures driving the diagnosis rather than a solely scientific and ethnographic approach.

Regarding the process of creating a diagnosis out of poor validity of research creates a confirmatory approach to researching the diagnosis. In the case of Gaming Addiction, this appears to be a primary concern for many researchers as many internet gaming screeners or approaches to classifying video game addiction through ratings employ this approach. By utilizing the idea of a diagnosis based upon unconfirmed and non-consensual nosology criterion, researchers are only confirming what has been iterated to them as a diagnosis, rather than conducting necessary and validating research based upon an ethnographic or theoretical approach. As a result, Aarseth et al. (2016) reports this type of thinking "lock[s] [research] into a confirmatory approach rather than an exploration of the boundaries of normal versus pathological" resulting in "more screening instruments (confirmatory thinking), instead of stimulating the fundamental validation and theoretical work (exploratory thinking) that is needed to understand the phenomenology of problematic gaming" (pg. 3).

This top-down approach to the idea of Gaming Addiction could eventually construe other pleasurable activities as an addiction as well (Aarseth et al, 2016; Bean et al., 2017). For instance, writing, playing outside with friends, dancing, or even running marathons could come under scrutiny as individuals who enjoy these past times fit the current DSM criteria. The lack of any phenomenological data on video gamers and the culture portrayed within the diagnostic category constitutes a real concern for researchers and clinicians. Utilizing an inductive reasoning or bottom-up approach, built upon clinical observation, case studies, ethnographic approaches, and video gamer culture would provide more compelling evidence of the ideology of Gaming Disorder.

With a multitude of varying clinical tests being developed and utilized across clinical practices clinicians are then faced with a difficult task of critically examining and choosing a test for Gaming Disorder from a variety of sources all with their own inherent flaws. Utilizing these tests, a clinician may then choose a test which is not psychometrically sound and/or has poor operational definitions. The lack of general consensus on symptomology, assessment, and use of appropriate and substantiated clinical pathology provides clinicians with a difficult task of evaluating the potential for a true diagnosis leading to the probability of false positives, mislabeling of healthy video gamers, and/or more clinical harm than good.

Flow

The concept of Flow was first named by Mihaly Csikszentmihalyi, but easily can be seen throughout other disciplines and even traced back to Eastern religious roots (Csikszentmihalyi, 2009). It is part of positive psychology and also known as "being in the zone." Flow is the mental state of operating or performing an activity in a fully immersed manner. While entranced, an individual enjoys a feeling of energizing focus, complete involvement in the activity, and immense enjoyment. It is not to be confused with the idea of hyper focus or only focusing on one aspect of an assignment, becoming sidetracked, or being "captured" to the forfeiture of other projects or activities. However, it is important to note that even though hyper focusing is usually seen as detrimental to individuals as there is a loss of productivity, this is not always the case. Hyper focusing upon a task or activity can be beneficial for completion, increased rewards, internal drives, and task orientation (Webb et al., 2016).

Csikszentmihalyi broke his concept into six factors of an experience of flow:

1.   Focused concentration on the present moment or task
2.   Merging of action and awareness
3.   A loss of reflective self-consciousness
4.   A sense of personal control or agency over the situation or activity
5.   A distortion of temporal experience or one's subjective experience of time is altered (sped up or down)
6.   Experience of the activity as intrinsically rewarding or as autotelic

These factors can be experienced individually and independently of one another, but only when combined together do they constitute the idea of flow.

Csikszentmihalyi further stated autotelic personalities tend to experience flow more often and in greater capacities than those who are not. An autotelic personality is one who completes task for their own sake in the current present moment rather than for a later goal. One cannot be autotelic completely as everyone has to complete tasks which are considered to be unenjoyable. However, there are graduations of autotelic ranging from none experienced to individuals who believe everything they do holds value and can be construed as fun. Autotelic individuals are considered to have specific personality traits such as curiosity, persistence, low self-centeredness, and intrinsic motivation. Csikszentmihalyi describes individuals who are considered to be autotelic to be individuals who need few material possessions, little entertainment, comfort, power over their situation, or fame due to their intrinsic feelings of reward from their experiences. For example, the artist who gets lost in their work and never sells a painting or the musician who plays for hours on end enjoying every second of the moment even when no one is listening. These are autotelic individuals whom live for the pleasure of their craft.

Flow has been considered to be one of the main reasons why individuals play video games. The idea is the game creates entertainment through intrinsic motivation of playing. It is believed that without the intrinsic motivation, one cannot enter a state of flow. This is thought to be created through the balance of skill and challenge of the game to which the video gamer's attention is engaged with high motivation to continue playing. It fosters an enjoyable experience which elicits the continuation of play. However, within the world of video gaming, motivation is not always intrinsic. It may start off intrinsic, but may eventually lead to extrinsic rewards. World of Warcraft has appeared to move to this style of play with video gamers being able to level their character for rewards, but then once the expansion is completed or they have managed to progress as far as possible, they begin or continue through daily quests. The internal motivation for the game becomes less noticeable and the sense of extrinsic rewards becomes more pronounced.

The Case for Immersion

Playing video games and becoming immersed has some similarities to the concept of flow, but also important and distinct differences. Immersion has been used to define the realism of video games and is linked to enjoyment of playing (Brown & Cairns, 2004). It may be seen as the equivalent of wearing "blinders" and only being able to see what is in front of one's self. Everything else outside of the undertaking appears to melt away and the focus becomes solely on the task at hand. Flow can provide a base for immersion, but is not inherently as deeply engrossed. Immersion is the concept of being immensely and intensely present while engaged within a task or activity which encompasses one's entire attention, but is built on past experiences, unlike flow, which focuses upon the present and does not require past familiarities with an activity. Furthermore, there is not always a sense of intrinsic purpose when playing a video game as there are achievements and other rewards for completing tasks or leveling up within the game as stated as a requirement for flow. These achievements may begin as intrinsic rewards and give a sense of accomplishment, but eventually fade to extrinsic motivations of rewards for completing tasks.

However, as immersion is important, one must have a schema in which to build on and become immersed. This is where flow can be of service. A state of flow is considered a basic schema to which one learns new cognitions and repeated encounters. As video gamers create and build the basic schemas for different video games and genres, they utilize the concept of flow to create and absorb the building blocks of the occurrence. However, once the schema has been created, flow is no longer needed to create the satisfaction and immersion takes over. It is of a similar process akin to unconsciously understanding archetypes. Genres of video games have similarities between them which places them in the same space of play and mechanisms. Once a specific genre or game draws a player towards it, they have already created the sense of flow by playing it before. However, when playing a genre after flow occurs and expectation of what the genre consists of, the video gamer immediately enters into immersion bypassing the state of flow.

This means the video gamer becomes completely absorbed into the video game through the ebb and flow of the narrative, the controls, the audio and visual components, and the actions on the screen. Within video games, the video gamer loses a sense of physical reality and becomes engrossed and immersed within the game, world, avatar, actions, environment, and controls of the character they are playing as. The game itself becomes psychically real for the individual and they place an importance of experiencing the sensations while being spatially located within the virtual avatar and the environment.

An example of this would be The Legend of Zelda (Nintendo, 1986–2017). The franchised series has spanned over three decades of video games totaling over 18 different games. Inherently, video gamers play a similar game each time they buy the new Legend of Zelda game. If the game is similar and plays comparable to the previous game, why are video gamers consistently buying it? The answer is immersion. The video gamer enjoys the content and becomes significantly engrossed and engaged with the components even though it is similar to its past predecessors. The flow of the first time they played created a base schema for them so they know what to expect in the new version. The idea that they will be playing a new game exists, but they enter a state of immersion due to having the schema in place which is a driving force to play the video game.

Many video gamers cite immersion as an important component of relating to the realism of the virtual world, sounds, experience, and depth of the storyline. It is considered to be a critical aspect of enjoyment of the video game (Douglas & Hargadon, 2000). It can be a "make or break" effect upon the video gamer based upon the game characteristics. For instance, if a video gamer sees an object not analogous to the scene, storyline, or area to which one is playing it, it can break the immersion effect. However, conversely, if the objects, scenery, and sounds are balanced, they can continue the immersion effect or even deepen it.

Video games are not the only intermediate which produces this effect, albeit technology mediums do enhance the capability, but reading an engrossing book, watching an intense movie, cooking a savory meal—all can be considered to be immersion based tasks after a base schema has been created. For video games, the immersion is much more intense and difficult to pull one's self out. This is due to the idea of sensory integration. Multiple sensory channels are being utilized from a video gamer's perspective, tactile by the controller, vision by the eyes and screen, and auditory by the sounds produced by the game.

Attempting to pull one's self out of such an experience can be daunting. The video gamer is continually processing the information through these channels and therefore becoming integrated deeper within the game itself. Parents who take the video game away or complain that their child is not listening to them when they are playing are not taking into consideration these immersion effects. Furthermore, when they do stop playing the game to complete a task or attend an appointment parents usually observe their children in a negative mood state or irritability. Putting down a book at a pivotal moment to take care of responsibilities or to stop watching a football game during overtime can easily create the same or similar irritability due to the break of the immersion. Indeed, stopping an action when one is engrossed and immersed within the task is likely to irritate the calmest and best adjusted individuals.

It is important to note that this is different from hyper focusing due to the possibility of losing the ability to pull one's self out of the process or losing focus on the task. With immersion, one does not lose the ability to focus upon the surroundings of the video game, the player becomes engrossed with them. The bird chirping, they hear it, the sword striking down upon an enemy, they feel it, the movement needed to run from another NPC, the player is experiencing it. During these moments, the player is using all senses to filter as much sensory information as possible, rapidly processing every move and sequentially planning out their next one. There is not a perception of detrimentally due to the constant bombardment of sensory information distinctively differing immersion from hyper focusing.

As Charlton (2002) pointed out, addiction measures of video game playing do not distinguish between high engagement with video games versus addiction, the concept of immersion is an important facet to consider. Indeed, Charlton stated through one of his studies on addiction versus high engagement:

> The existence of milder and stronger criteria for pathological computing behavior, with the former also indicating high engagement, implies that people who are classified as computer dependent or computer

addicted might often be more accurately said to be highly computer engaged.

(pg. 19)

Highly engaged individuals do not constitute an addiction framework to work off of, whereas rethinking the idea of highly engaged individuals as immersed can be utilized for clinical work. Reclassifying video gamers into the arena of immersed over addicted can provide a change to the clinical application of video games in a therapeutic context. Video gamers are familiar with the context of immersion as they freely use the terminology to describe and discuss video games. This creates an amenable experience within the therapeutic atmosphere and does not subjectively interfere with the clinical work. It helps to build rapport and additionally opens up dialogues about the video games being played, further germinating the ability to learn about the archetypal experience of the video gamer.

References

Aarseth, E., Bean, A. M., Boonen, H., Colder Carras, M., Coulson, M., Das, D., . . . vanRooij, A. J. (2016). Scholars' open debate paper on the World Health Organization ICD-11 Gaming Disorder proposal. *Journal of Behavioral Addictions*. Advance online publication. http://dx.doi.org/ 10.1556/2006.5.2016.088

Abbasi, A. Z., Ting, D. H., & Hlavacs, H. (2017). Engagement in Games: Developing an Instrument to Measure Consumer Videogame Engagement and Its Validation. *International Journal of Computer Games Technology, 4*, 1–10.

American Psychiatric Association (APA). (2013). *Diagnostic and statistical manual of mental disorders: DSM–5*. Washington, DC: American Psychiatric Association.

American Psychiatric Association (APA). (2018). APA Media Psychology and Technology Division (Div 46) Policy Statement. Retrieved from https://www.scribd.com/document/ 374879861/APA-Media-Psychology-and-Technology-Division-Div-46-Policy-Statement-Expressing-Concern-Regarding-the-Plan-to-Include-Gaming-Disorder-in-the-ICD-1.

Bean, A. M., Nielsen, R. K. L., van Rooij, A. J., & Ferguson, C. J. (2017). Video game addiction: The push to pathologize video games. *Professional Psychology: Research and Practice*. Advance online publication. Http://dx.doi.org/10.1037/pro0000150

Brown, E., & Cairns, P. (2004). A grounded investigation of game immersion. Proceedings of CHI '04 Extended Abstracts on Human Factors in Computing Systems (pp. 1297–1300). New York: ACM. doi:10.1145/985921.986048

Carbonell, X. (2017). From Pong to Pokemon Go, catching the essence of the Internet Gaming Disorder diagnosis. *Journal of Behavioral Addictions*. Advance online publication. http://dx.doi.org/10.1556/2006.6 .2017.010

Charlton, J. P. (2002). A factor-analytic investigation of computer 'addiction' and engagement. *British Journal of Psychology, 93*, 329–344. http://dx.doi.org/10.1348/ 000712602760146242

Charlton, J. P., & Danforth, I. D. W. (2007). Distinguishing addiction and high engagement in the context of online game playing. *Computers in Human Behavior, 23*, 1531–1548. http://dx.doi.org/10.1016/j.chb.2005 .07.002

Csikszentmihalyi, M. (2009). *Flow: The psychology of optimal experience.* New York: Harper and Row.

Douglas, Y., & Hargadon, A. (2000) The pleasure principle: Immersion, engagement, flow. ACM, 153–160.

Duggan, M. (2015). *Gaming and gamers.* Washington, DC: Pew Research Center. Retrieved from www.pewinternet.org/2015/12/15/gamingand-gamers/

Gentile, D. (2009). Pathological video-game use among youth ages 8 to 18: A national study. *Psychological Science, 20,* 594–602. http://dx.doi.org/ 10.1111/j.1467–9280. 2009.02340.x

Griffiths, M. D. (1991). Amusement machine playing in childhood and adolescence: A comparative analysis of video games and fruit machines. *Journal of Adolescence, 14,* 53–73. http://dx.doi.org/10.1016/01401971(91)90045-S

Griffiths, M. D. (2000). Does internet and computer "addiction" exist? Some case study evidence. *Cyberpsychology, Behavior, and Social Networking, 3*, 211–218. http://dx.doi.org/ 10.1089/109493100316067

Griffiths, M. D. (2008). Videogame addiction: Further thoughts and observations. *International Journal of Mental Health and Addiction, 6,* 182–185. http://dx.doi.org/ 10.1007/s11469–007–9128-y

Griffiths, M. D., van Rooij, A. J., Kardefelt-Winther, D., Starcevic, V., Király, O., Pallesen, S.,. . .Demetrovics, Z. (2016). Working towards an international consensus on criteria for assessing internet gaming disorder: A critical commentary on Petry et al. (2014). *Addiction, 111,* 167–175. http://dx.doi.org/10.1111/add.13057

Kardefelt-Winther, D. (2016). Proposal for deletion. Retrieved from http://apps.who.int/ classifications/icd11/browse/proposals/l-m/en#/http://id.who.int/icd/entity/ 1448597234?readOnly=true&action=DeleteEntityProposal&stableProposalGroupId= 1cda9b24–6fc9–40bd-b529-d 3e8e8a1e3b1.

Kazdin, A. E. (2008). Evidence-based treatment and practice: New opportunities to bridge clinical research and practice, enhance the knowledge base, and improve patient care. *American Psychologist, 63*(3), 146–159.

King, D.L., & Delfabbro, P.H. (2014). Internet gaming disorder treatment: A review of definitions of diagnosis and treatment outcome. *Journal of Clinical Psychology, 70,* 942–955. http://dx.doi.org/10.1002/jclp.22097

King, D. L., Haagsma, M. C., Delfabbro, P. H., Gradisar, M., & Griffiths, M. D. (2013). Toward a consensus definition of pathological videogaming: A systematic review of psychometric assessment tools. *Clinical Psychology Review, 33,* 331–342. http://dx.doi.org/ 10.1016/j.cpr.2013 .01.002

Krossbakken, E., Pallesen, S., Molde, H., Mentzoni, R. A., & Finserås, T. R. (2017). Not good enough? Further comments to the wording, meaning, and the conceptualization of Internet Gaming Disorder. *Journal of Behavioral Addictions.* Advance online publication. http://dx.doi .org/10.1556/2006.6.2017.013

Kuss, D. J., Griffiths, M. D., & Pontes, H. M. (2016). Chaos and confusion in DSM–5 diagnosis of Internet Gaming Disorder: Issues, concerns, and recommendations for clarity in the field. *Journal of Behavioral Addictions.* Advance online publication. http://dx.doi.org/10.1556/2006.5 .2016.062

Mental Health TAG (2017). Content enhancement proposal. Retrieved from http://apps.who.int/classifications/icd11/browse/proposals/f/en#/http://id.who.int/icd/entity/1448597234?readOnly=true&action=ContentEnhancementProposal&stable ProposalGroupId=6f3271a4-aab6-4a2c-87ec-3e766593f528.

Nintendo. (1986). The Legend of Zelda. [video game]. Kyoto, Japan: Nintendo.

Nintendo. (1987). Zelda II: The Adventure [video game]. Kyoto, Japan: Nintendo.

Nintendo. (1992). The Legend of Zelda: A Link to the Past [video game]. Kyoto, Japan: Nintendo.

Nintendo. (1998). The Legend of Zelda: Ocarina of Time [video game]. Kyoto, Japan: Nintendo.

Nintendo. (2000). The Legend of Zelda: Majora's Mask [video game]. Kyoto, Japan: Nintendo.

Nintendo. (2003). The Legend of Zelda: The Wind Waker [video game]. Kyoto, Japan: Nintendo.

Nintendo. (2006). The Legend of Zelda: Twilight Princess [video game]. Kyoto, Japan: Nintendo.

Nintendo. (2011). The Legend of Zelda: Skyward Sword [video game]. Kyoto, Japan: Nintendo.

Nintendo. (2017). The Legend of Zelda: Breath of the Wild [video game]. Kyoto, Japan: Nintendo.

Petry, N. M., Rehbein, F., Gentile, D. A., Lemmens, J. S., Rumpf, H. J., Mößle, T., . . . O'Brien, C. P. (2014). An international consensus for assessing internet gaming disorder using the new DSM–5 approach. *Addiction, 109,* 1399–1406. http://dx.doi.org/10.1111/add.12457

Przybylski, A., Weinstein, N., & Murayama, K. (2017). Internet gaming disorder: Investigating the clinical relevance of a new phenomenon. *The American Journal of Psychiatry, 174,* 230–236.

Quandt, T. (2017). Stepping back to advance: Why IGD needs an intensified debate instead of a consensus. *Journal of Behavioral Addictions.* Advance online publication. http://dx.doi.org/10.1556/2006.6.2017.014

Teachman, B. A., Drabick, D. A. G., Hershenberg, R., Goldfried, M. R., Vivian, D., & Wolfe, B. E. (2013). Bridging the gap between clinical research and clinical practice: Introduction to the special section. *Psychotherapy, 49,* 2, 97–100.

van Rooij, A. J., & Prause, N. (2014). A critical review of "Internet addiction" criteria with suggestions for the future. *Journal of Behavioral Addictions, 3,* 203–213. http://dx.doi.org/10.1556/JBA.3.2014.4.1

van Rooij, A. J., van Looy, J., & Billieux, J. (2016). Internet Gaming Disorder as a formative construct: Implications for conceptualization and measurement. *Psychiatry and Clinical Neurosciences.* Advance online publication. http://dx.doi.org/10.1111/pcn.12404

van Rooij, A.J., & Kardefelt-Winther, D.(2017). Lost in the chaos: Flawed literature should not generate new disorders. *Journal of Behavioral Addictions.* Advance online publication. http://dx.doi.org/10.1556/2006 .6.2017.015

van Rooij, A. J., Schoenmakers, T. M., & van de Mheen, D. (2017). Clinical validation of the C-VAT 2.0 assessment tool for gaming disorder: A sensitivity analysis of the proposed DSM–5 criteria and the clinical characteristics of young patients with "video game addiction." *Addictive Behaviors, 64,* 269–274. http://dx.doi.org/10.1016/j.addbeh .2015.10.018

Webb, J. T., Amend, E. R., Webb, N. E., Goerss, J., Beljan, P., & Olenchak, R.F. (2016). *Misdiagnosis and dual diagnoses of gifted children and adults: ADHD, bipolar, OCD, Asperger's, depression, and other disorders*. Tucson, AZ: Great Potential Press.

World Health Organization (WHO). (2016a). Gaming disorder proposal. Retrieved from http://apps.who.int/classifications/icd11/browse/proposals/l-m/en#/http://id.who.int/icd/entity/1602669465?readOnlytrue&actionAdd NewEntityProposal&stable ProposalGroupId47bfdbcd-524a-4af7a179–02f29517f23a

World Health Organization (WHO). (2016b). Hazardous gaming proposal. Retrieved from http://apps.who.int/classifications/icd11/browse/proposals/ l-m/en#/http://id.who.int/icd/entity/1602669465?readOnlytrue&action AddNewEntityProposal&stable ProposalGroupId93aeefc3-b9e2–43b7abd1–2ca742d70a79

Working Therapeutically with with Video Gamers

10

While most current guides to therapy lay out a step-by-step instruction manual for clinicians to follow within a therapeutic setting, this book does not subscribe to that philosophy. The primary reason is because it creates a mindless and drone-like mentality and implementation to the practice of psychology and therapy. Armed with appropriate knowledge, a clinician can use that same awareness where they best see fit, which humanizes the experience rather than following a laid-out script. If an outline or decision tree is created with the instructions to follow it closely, then one is no longer working therapeutically, but following blindly. The point of using archetypes, video games, and virtual worlds together is to work with video gamers based upon their experience and the clinician's aptitude. This book provides the information necessary to do just that.

The culmination of this book and its contents is this chapter. Working with video gamers is an experience to behold when the clinician is open to the client's worldview and interested not just in their words, but in the worlds in which they play. Video games are another world, but just like work at the end of the day, video gamers must stop and come back to reality; however, when they are playing the video game they are indeed working with their minds and imagination. Utilizing this knowledge, clinicians are appropriately armed with not just an interworking of video games, but the ability to respond critically, yet clearly, to the clients in front of them. By having the ability to respond to the client's video gaming habits from a multitude of perspectives, rapport is gathered quicker, clients feel as if they are being heard, and the progress of clinical therapy ensues. The client is the expert on how and why they play video games. Clinicians are the mirror for clients to discover the draw of the game and understand more about themselves while working on other difficulties.

Clinical researchers to date have incorporated cognitive and play therapy interventions for the treatment of video gamers showing improvements in adaptive functioning suggesting other perspectives outside of addiction can be viable (Adal, 2013; Harpur, Lawlor, & Fitzgerald, 2006; Van, 2014). However, they appear to suffer from a lack of integration of video game knowledge and character development which normally is extremely important in understanding different cultures—in this case video gamer ethos. As therapists are presumed to be experts in communication, it makes sense to utilize the language of the video game world to communicate and understand where the client may be presently situated. Utilizing this immersive experience opens the door for a more collaborative therapy, increasing communication about video games, playing, and extrapolating players' experiences into real life contexts.

While a cognitive behavioral approach would emphasize a focus on irrational cognitions and dichotomous thinking it would leave the importance of virtual experience out of the process. The different experiences via playing the video game can be further discussed in therapeutic sessions increasing rapport, engagement, and greater understanding of the habits of the client. By asking questions and requesting attention be placed in certain areas, an individual can learn more about themselves, their video game habits, and why they play certain roles. It additionally opens up dialogue about the virtual world and the player's interest instead of subjectively deciding an individual's behavior to be behaviorally maladaptive. As such, the therapist does not become entrapped by the addiction paradigm of thought and can constructively approach the topic in an effort to learn more about the client's experience and virtual worlds.

Understanding Virtual Worlds

When a client comes into the office from a referral source stating he/she is addicted to video games, the clinician should take an analytical approach to the specific referral statement. The first question should be similar to the extent of "what makes you think you're addicted?" Therapists are trained to clinically and critically think about a client's nature and what may be troubling them. However, when one sees the concept of video game addiction coming through on paperwork or from the mouths of parents, ones predisposition to what is heard throughout the news media and other sources. This does not entail critical thinking of a topic and can easily misinform the modality of treatment and manners in which treatment ensues.

The beginning chapters laid out the different ideas of what constitutes a video game, going into great detail about the different genres, motivations, and personality formulations of the video gamer. As such, it is considered to be a primer of sorts to the world of video gaming. By now you will have an increased knowledge of the video game world due to the previously presented material. As a result, you as the reader should have much more than a basic understanding of what constitutes video games and the players who play them. The video gamer in front of the clinician will undoubtedly appreciate this knowledge and continue the enlightenment process through their discussions of the video games. This is likely due to the safe feeling of the therapeutic milieu created by the clinician.

When a client talks about playing a video game which entails rapid movements, rushing around the screen, and using guns to defeat others in a battle arena, the first thought should be that the client is playing an action video game. If a client discusses their love of a character due to being able to pick and choose abilities and play a long storyline, the genre of the video game coming to mind should be a role-playing video game. If the conversation flows around building a world, creation, and managing multiple items or abilities within a game, simulations are likely the type of game being played. By listening to the content of the world from the video gamer and asking questions about the types of games being played, the genre of enjoyment comes into focus. This is always the first step when working with video gamers because the characters found within the genres usually are specific to the genre played and inform the clinician of what clinical work needs to be done. Understanding the virtual world in which one plays is of the upmost importance of understand where the client is at.

Acknowledging Biases

Unless you, as the clinician, were born into the world of video games, it is likely that there are biases being held about working with video gamers. As research has shown in the area of video games and elder clinicians, they tend to be biased against video games and video gamers (Ferguson, 2015). This is not a difficult problem to overcome for the clinician as the training received has prepared clinicians to continuously examine their own beliefs and biases to not introduce them to their clients. Indeed, this may seem like a daunting task at times when the client comes in and has not progressed much since the previous session. However, everyone progresses at different and varying paces—and this includes video gamers. It is important to not be held by societal beliefs as each person is an individual and is psychically different from one another.

Integrating the knowledge in this book into the therapy sessions is a must. The ability to use it easily surprises most clinicians and garners the client's trust quicker. The integration of video games, psychology, and therapy is crucial to understanding the ethos of the video gamer and how they have come to be who they are. Video game culture is a unique one, springing out of geek and nerd culture. It is seen as being on the outskirts of society, but has a deep and rich history—never mind a strong and knowledgeable following. If the previous statement doesn't hold true for the reader, I would suggest attending one of the many conventions held around the United States and the world which gamers, geeks, and nerds attend by the thousands. It will be sure to change the most skeptical mind.

Video gamers may communicate through the means of fantasy worlds, but that should not hold any clinician back, as fantasy is important to human development and understanding. Everyday millions of people interact with one another via online communications whether it be Facebook, texting, video games, or even Twitter. Fantasy worlds are a boon for clinician surveillance of how the client is working through difficult moments of life. The actions completed within the game, the type of avatar played, the personality domains the client is high or low in, and the gamer's online offline self are intensely entangled with one another and provide exceptionally rich data. This data is impressively important to understand the mental bases video gamers are working with, and can be additionally useful instruments to be used as interventions.

As for the personal biases against video gamers, clinicians must work on them just as much as clients work on their own difficulties. A good place to start is to label and realistically confront personal biases in writing, in session with the client, or cognitively. It is likely that the video gamer in front of the clinician has them about therapy as well. Creating an open space to have a dialogue about the concerns which do appear in therapeutic sessions to behaviors which clients present with is one of the easiest ways to confront them. Involving the client in these dialogues with statements like "I am not sure about what you mean by ___, can you elaborate some more?" Or "this is not within my area of knowledge, help me understand what you mean by ___." Even, "help me understand more about your world as I am not familiar with it" can be useful. Openly acknowledging any possible bias you have about video games with the client changes the dynamic between you and the client for the better.

Meaningful Imaginative Play

When video gamers engage in their choice of play they are creating a meaningful experience. This experience has to be investigated further. As play and video games are intertwined, yet include role playing, creativity, and non-literal behaviors, understanding motivations for choices made within the virtual world is inherent to working with clients. Video gamers are making meaning out of their choice of games and mannerisms of play. Gamers who utilizes a strong hold manner which one barricades themselves inside of their compound and do not venture very far *outside* in order to build up resources in a strategy game is playing defensively. Likely, there are defensive mannerisms in their approach to the world outside of the game. The video gamer prospectively believes that by playing through a defensive position, they can outlast what is attacking them. Obviously in a video game this may be true, but outside of the game, likely not. However, this behavior becomes ingrained due to the success the video gamer has had within the game. It becomes the job for the clinician to shed light upon that behavior and the incongruences between them and reality.

Through the meaningful interactions experienced through video games narrative play is experienced. This type of play is exceptionally important to the video gamer and the game being played. To disrupt the meaning behind the experience is essentially to tell video gamers their experiences are not deemed worthy. Video games have stories which elicit emotional content and can be remarkably useful in providing a clarification to an intervention or creating a space to process difficult emotions. For instance, in Chapter 8, Final Fantasy was discussed, specifically the moment when Aerith was killed by another character within the game. There is no way to stop this from occurring, yet video gamers surely attempted. Usually one can load the last saved file or restart the mission if they lose a beloved character, but not in the case of Aerith. In order to progress, she must perish. At this time of the game, the character has developed an attachment to Aerith and easily becomes saddened by the loss of her. Having another person tell the video gamer that it was a fictional character and they should not be saddened because she really wasn't alive demeans the entire emotional atmosphere endured. Instead it should be explored how the loss of the character played a role in one's life and offers a teachable moment to talk about loss and grief. These moments occur throughout the storylines of many diverse games and offer much in return for exploring them with the client.

Archetypal Play

The archetypes outlined in this book are primary archetypes which can be found across all video games. Clearly there are many more, but the ones listed are considered to be principal ones. While other archetypes may be present and there are definitely mixtures of the archetypal characters, they all generate from these primary ones. Talking with clients about their choice in archetypal play is an important part of the therapeutic process. While the emotional content and genres are the beginnings of the conversation and are additionally important, the archetypes are even more so. Archetypes have a deeper connection to the personality and being of the video gamer. Examining the archetypes played throughout the differing video games reveals a pattern of preferred play. The video gamer usually chooses to play primarily as one or two of the archetypes listed. On occasion video gamers play more than one or two types, creating a hybrid.

The chosen archetype has a distinct importance about the client and involves one's own sense of being, self, personality, and environments. Learning more about each archetype and the involvement within the person in game and outside of the virtual realm tells a story about the individual. If a video gamer chooses to play as a warrior, chances are he/she may have a need or want to protect others and/or may need some help understanding their interpersonal relationships and skills. A healer may give too much to others without giving time to their own needs. Rogues don't like to be seen, similar to ranged combat, and strike from a distance, but likely have anxiety symptoms when directly confronted. Each of these different approaches to playing the video game works in their own unique ways to complete it, but the video gamer may not have the ability outside of the game thus requiring the clinician's help to understand the concepts and choices in a different light and manner.

Video gamers who do not like to be confronted or have anxiety in provocative moments can manage in the game due to their abilities, but require additional help for the moment when they are not able to stay ranged (if playing a ranged character) or are faced with an overpowering force and have to deal with the conflict. The therapist can give the video gamers the tools, but also relate their abilities back to their characters' combative qualities. The warrior who is always being a savior for others, but not him/herself requires stronger adaptability and boundaries when dealing with others who may rely on him/her for that savior ability. Same goes for the healer mentioned above, better boundaries and more time for one's self. The archetype played gives the clinician insight into what needs to be worked on, a deeper understanding of the psychological concepts of the client, and direction in which to psychically move the client forward with their own interworking and games played.

Do Not Be Discouraged

Working with video gamers is not an easy task at times. Utilizing their own experiences and attempting to promote change is not always a quick or steady process. Many hang-ups with the therapeutic process do occur at inopportune times. It is similar to how other processes with clients can be utilizing other modalities of treatment. For example, if a client is being resistant towards change and actively defying positive growth in Jungian transformative principles, ignoring rational thoughts for irrational ones with Cognitive Behavioral, or even if a clinician is not appropriately utilizing humanistic principles when working with clients such as being judgmental. During these moments, little progress is made versus other times where it is made by leaps and bounds. Jumping into working with video gamers can be quite confusing if one does not have a strong background in the terminology, games played, and what a client means when they say MMORPG. Stay curious and continue the work as the video gamer will help with parts which may need some light shined upon them. Just like riding a bike, over time it becomes easier and quicker.

   Video games can be utilized as a main form of treatment inside and outside of the therapeutic setting to increase personal growth and abilities of the video gamer. Creating a more holistic understanding for the video gamer balanced with psychology, clinical ability, and appropriate background in video games brings about improvement across many environments. Utilizing the virtual worlds and concepts found within to increase personal abilities and then overlay them upon real life difficulties is a worthy task. As a clinician, the knowledge and understanding shown to the video gamer brings about the trust and change sought after. Video gamers are able to transfer the material learned via the virtual worlds, characters, interactions, and other various actions into their other environments utilizing tools procured by the clinician. Incorporating virtual realms into the therapeutic process is a crucial undertaking when working with video gamers which helps build the confidence to move outside of the video games and use what skills have already been learned. Becoming knowledgeable of video games and how they can be used is the first step in which to engage the client appropriately without judgment. This may include briefly learning about the different gameplay, character developments, and linear storyline uniquely found in each video game or even consulting with video game experts.

References

Adal, J. (2013). Bringing play therapy into the new millennium: Incorporating video game technology into mental health treatment.

Ferguson, C. J. (2015). Clinicians' attitudes toward video games vary as a function of age, gender and negative beliefs about youth: A sociology of media research approach. *Computers in Human Behavior, 52*, 379–386. http://dx.doi.org/10.1016/j.chb.2015.06.016

Harpur, J., Lawlor, M., & Fitzgerald, M. (2006). *Succeeding with interventions for Asperger syndrome adolescents: A guide to communication and socialisation in interaction therapy.* London: Jessica Kingsley Publishers.

Van, B. B.(2014). *Treating video game addiction: Three brief sessions.* Alexandria, VA: American Counseling Association.

For the Families! Guiding Ideas and Resources for Therapists and Families

11

Here are some guiding principles and common questions that may help parents and therapists implement discussions on video games in the home or office. Parents are usually concerned that playing video games can cause their children to become addicted, sociopaths, or even distempered to growing up and facing reality. Questions, concerns, and common misconceptions arise in private practices, from families, and society about video games, video gamers, and what the possible impact they may have upon the players. This chapter additionally contains some tools which have been useful in therapy to work with the video gamer in understanding their characters, the world around them, and also with management of difficult situations.

My child plays video games after school with friends, I am worried they will not be social outside of their video games

Video games allow the imagination to grow and take root in the player's experience of life. There are instances where video game players have taken the concepts found within the video game itself and used them in their own lives in order to obtain a goal. Furthermore, there are varying developmental stages in which children and adolescents grow, change, and develop their skills socially and interpersonally. Video games provide a safe place for these instances to take place and allow the child or adolescent to practice the social relationships building upon their interpersonal dynamics. The virtual world also provides a safe place for the video gamer to experience different emotional content and friendships. It is also important to not invalidate their companionships from games played online as, even though they may not know one another face-to-face, they still are friends. By stating "they are not real friends" it provides an invalidation of the player's experience and can do more harm than good to their emotional state and psyche.

How much screen time is too much screen time?

Researchers do not have an answer for this question, as much of the research is convoluted and not clear on the impact of video games or screen time. Former statements on the topic have been retracted often and continue to change. Psychologists and medical professionals attempt to err on the side of caution when examining this question. For now, we do not have any definitive answer on what can be construed as "too much gaming." The American Academy of Pediatrics has recently changed their guidelines and have become more family centered on their suggestions. Clinicians base their work in this area on the suggestion that the family and caregivers develop a plan that takes into account the dynamics of each family member in order to determine the best course of action.

However, there are instances where the child or adolescent may play too many video games and neglect other aspects of their lives. It is important to impose some form of limitation before the video gamer can proceed with their gaming time. If a parent or caregiver begins to see changes in mood, such as irritation, then it may be important to set stricter limits until the video gamer can manage their own emotional moods proficiently. Setting boundaries is the best course of action and an important one for all families to implement, not just with video games, but all instances where a child or adolescent may be having difficulties with any activity. Having a conversation about limits and encouraging the child to be a part of the conversation is exceptionally important. Children and adolescents require guidance and nurturing of course, but encouraging the child to be a part of the conversation allows them to have a lasting impact and begins their participation in the concept of setting their own limits in all activities of life. When parents set the limits without a conversation or explanation, it can interfere with the child's ability to do the same in the future. It is additionally important to ensure that the parents and caregivers are appropriately modeling behavior as well so children can learn from the people they are around the most—family.

Video game addiction is everywhere! Sound the alarm and get these kids help!

Video game addiction is not an actual disorder, but the term is used fairly often in society. It is a proposed disorder in the psychological models of thinking; however, if we look closely at their perceived criteria, one can see their models are currently unsubstantiated and not approached from an ethnographic standpoint. This means they are determined by a confirmatory approach which only confirms what one is looking for, not whether the current criteria is actually correct. The concept of video game addiction is far from accurate with percentages in the 30–50%. These studies are usually poorly constructed, misconstrue high engagement with addiction, and variables examined are not usually a clear picture or indication of what the participants are experiencing. Examining studies which take these variables into consideration with more appropriate experimental designs shows that the rate is closer to 1–2% of the video gamer population. What is even more concerning is the attempt at diagnosing a condition which is fairly misunderstood as researchers are not in a majority of consensus on what the proposed disorder is attempting to do.

Playing violent video games will make my child violent!

Hundreds of scientific studies have been conducted on the topic of violent video games and violent acts committed; these studies convincingly evaluated and found that there was no relationship between these variables. What they did find is that playing violent video games has shown small and very short-term rises in aggression, but that they are short lived; the player could be violent the first few minutes after stopping video game play but did not persist into long term aggression or violence. In fact, as video games have become more violent and consumption of these games has risen, the over-all violence rates have dropped significantly across the nation. As a result, a majority of researchers have concluded that there are no significant links between violent video game play, aggression, and violence committed by video gamers.

Other research that has been of importance to society is whether violent video games desensitize video gamers to violence. Emerging research has debunked this as well. The research showed humans have the ability to differentiate between real world violence and video game violence, although developmentally the ability to appropriately differentiate between the two begins around the age of 7. This is why there are rating systems incorporated into the gaming industry. Embracing age limits and restrictions makes video games safer for children. This means a player with a developed brain may kill, steal from, or hurt another individual in the video game, but they are not going to commit the same acts outside of the video game because morally they understand the differences between the two.

My kids play video games all the time and I am afraid that they will fall cognitively, interpersonally, and physically behind

We have no real evidence that shows video gamers are cognitively or physically deficient. A more likely probing of the situation would reveal poor eating habits and a lack of exercise within the child's immediate environments. There are ways to manage these difficulties appropriately such as choosing video games requiring physical exertion as they have been shown to increase physical activity and in some cases help people lose weight. Speaking cognitively, research around the topic of cognitive and intellectual abilities of video gamers have shown that playing these games can have a multitude of positive aspects associated with the play. For instance: video games have been shown to increase frustration tolerance, foster teamwork and cooperative play, build interpersonal relationships and skills, facilitate goal setting and task persistence, foster identity formation, learning, leadership, and develop a range of visual-spatial skills. Indeed there are many positive aspects of video gaming, but parents need to guide their children so they can reach the maximum benefits. How much time to do the children spend playing, are school grades appropriate, can the skills be extrapolated into real life situations, appropriate building of the tolerance and so on. This is where appropriate boundaries at home come into play along with the guidance of a trained therapist to help the family understand the concepts and implementation.

Do video games cause depression, anxiety, or ADHD?

A very common question to be asked in therapeutic settings for sure. First, there is no evidence that video games cause depression, anxiety, or ADHD. We do have scientific evidence that video gamers with these conditions appear to be attracted to video games as a way to cope with their conditions. For instance, a person with social isolation due to an illness or lack of immediate community will reach out to friends in video games for support and help with difficulties. A person who may be observed as anxious in real-life environments may feel safer interpersonally developing relationships across the virtual spaces which may calm anxious feelings. While a person who has ADHD-like symptoms or diagnosis will play video games because the ability to focus on the game, playing can improve attention and reduce impulsivity. Overall, these studies have shown video games provide a quite beneficial coping ability for those struggling with mental health. In a nutshell, video games have the ability to help with these difficulties rather than cause them, but should not be used as the sole method to cope with emotions— anything without moderation can be detrimental.

My child will become a bully due to playing video games

Video games have the ability to make people feel very powerful through their character and archetypal play. With great power always comes great responsibility. Those who choose to misuse power become villains. These powerful feelings are great to have and can influence the player to feel just as powerful in real life while increasing self-esteem. Sometimes those powerful emotions can bleed over into real life and video gamers feel as if they can take on the world. Research has shown that video games can reinforce some beliefs in the short-term for example bullying, sexism and misogynistic discussions and content within video games have not been able to shown to cause corresponding real life behavior in video gamers who are not already sexist or bullies. What this means is that these concepts and moral difficulties found online and in real life are not a result of video games, but are already present in the individual playing the game. They may be exacerbated for a brief moment after playing the game, but are not long lasting pending a person's moral code and personality. It is important to talk to children about discrimination towards other individuals regardless of gender, orientation, or ethnicity. It should never be acceptable to watch another individual suffer or be bullied by another individual and sit idly doing nothing to protect another individual. Teach children and adolescents that taking a stand against these prejudices and behaviors is the correct and moral way to approach the subject.

Resources for Parents and Clinicians

Entertainment Software Rating Board

The Entertainment Software Rating Board (ESRB) is the non-profit, self-regulatory body that assigns age and content ratings to video games and apps so consumers, especially parents, can make more informed decisions for their children and family. The ESRB rating system consists of three core components:

- Rating Categories: suggest age appropriateness via one of the six rating icons included in the table below
- Content Descriptors: indicate content that may have triggered a particular rating and/or may be of interest or concern (e.g. violence, language, suggestive themes and others.)
- Interactive Elements: inform about interactive aspects of a product, including the users' ability to interact, the sharing of users' location with others, if in-app purchases of digital goods are completed, and/or if unrestricted internet access is provided

Ratings assigned to physical (boxed) games also have rating summaries, which provide a more detailed description of the content that factored into the rating assigned.

Complete rating information for virtually all video games can be found on esrb.org and in the ESRB rating search app for smartphones and tablets (available in Google Play, the Apple App Store, and the Amazon App Store). Its website provides handy resource guides in the ESRB Parent Resources Center including step-by-step instructions for setting parental controls for video game consoles.

According to the Federal Trade Commission, the video game industry "continues to have the strongest self-regulatory code and enforcement of restrictions on marketing, advertising and selling mature-rated games to

Table 11.1 ESRB Categories

Rating Category	Description of Category
EARLY CHILDHOOD **eC** ESRB	Content is intended for young children.
EVERYONE **E** ESRB	Content is generally suitable for all ages. May contain minimal cartoon, fantasy or mild violence and/or infrequent use of mild language.
EVERYONE 10+ **E** 10+ ESRB	Content is generally suitable for ages 10 and up. May contain more cartoon, fantasy or mild violence, mild language and/or minimal suggestive theme.
TEEN **T** ESRB	Content is generally suitable for ages 13 and up. May contain violence, suggestive themes, crude humor, minimal blood, simulated gambling and/or infrequent use of strong language.
MATURE 17+ **M** ESRB	Content is generally suitable for ages 17 and up. May contain intense violence, blood and gore, sexual content and/or strong language.
ADULTS ONLY 18+ **A** ESRB	Content suitable only for adults ages 18 and up. May include prolonged scenes of intense violence, graphic sexual content and/or gambling with real currency.

Artwork by ESRB, used with permission.

younger audiences." Additionally, in 2011 the United States Supreme Court noted in its decision for Brown v. ESA that the ESRB rating system "does much to ensure that minors cannot purchase seriously violent games on their own, and that parents who care about the matter can readily evaluate the games their children bring home."

Leveling Up

Children and adolescents get "grounded" or disciplined often throughout their lives and parents are always wondering how to approach the topic of video games and discipline. Luckily there are tactics which work such as taking the system or game away, but a smart kid, and there are plenty of those, will figure out how to get around these punishments by obtaining a new cord, controller, or even in some cases a copy of the game from a friend in order to continue playing. What is usually suggested is that the parents find a safe place for the entire system or desktop which the child has no access to without their help. However, then the question arises of when would be an appropriate time to give the items back. Fortunately there are creative parents who have found ways to use video game mechanics against their children for punishment while getting chores completed as well for those busy parents. The following is an example which is used in my practice quite frequently and has really positive outcomes for the family and can easily be tailored to any age or situation.

These are examples of chores which can be completed around the house in order to work through the punishment and obtain their video games back. The important thing to remember is not to make the points too much to be able to get ungrounded quickly, but to also not make them too little in order to have the child completely ignore the exercise. Finding the middle ground of these chores and their value should be a discussion with the family to determine their worth.

Child's Play

Child's Play is a charitable organization (www.childsplaycharity.org) which has immense backing in order to seek improvement for children in hospitals and domestic violence shelters across the world. They are backed by many corporate sponsors from the video game industry and have even teamed up with EEDAR, a specialty video game research firm. EEDAR has a massive

Table 11.2 Leveling Up Behaviors Through Video Game Mechanics

CONGRATULATIONS, YOU'VE BEEN GROUNDED!

In order to get ungrounded you must earn _____ points!

Offense _____

Chore/Task	Point Value
Complete 1 load of laundry (washing and drying)	100
Walk the dog	20
Clean your room	50
Load dishwasher	25
Mow the lawn	50
Clean off counters and wash them	25
Clean our microwave	25
Wash windows	50
Sweep and mop kitchen	30
Dust 1 room of the house	30
Take out the trash and insert a new bag	20
Clean litter box	30
Empty the dishwasher	25
Clean the bathroom	30
Clean baseboards in 1 room	25
Vacuum 1 room	25
Prepare dinner	50
Take a walk with the family	50

Table 11.3 Child's Play Game Guide

Symptom Category	Ages Under 12	Ages 12 and Older
Pain	Mario Kart Space Invader Super Mario Galaxy Sonic All Stars Lego Games Plants VS Zombies	Space Invaders Rayman Origins Super Smash Brothers Pac-Man Street Fighter Shovel Knight
Short-Term Boredom	Mario Kart Super Mario Brother Wii Sports Peggle Angry Birds Tetris	Space Invaders Bomberman Super Smash Brothers NBA Jam Street Fighter MotorStorm RC
Long-Term Boredom	Mario & Luigi Pikimin Lego Games Minecraft Little Big Planet Super Paper Mario	Chrono Trigger The Legend of Zelda Monster Hunter Portal 2 Civilization Series Scribblenauts
Anxiety / Hyperactivity	Nintendogs Harvest Moon Zoo Tycoon Peggle Flower Lego Games	Scribblenauts Ducktales Viva Pinata Fluidity Wii Sports The Legend of Zelda
Sadness	Super Mario Brothers Kirby Rabbids Peggle Little Big Planet Adventure Time	Super Mario 64 Rayman Origins Mario Kart Splatoon Joe Danger Octodad
Cognitive Impairment	Nintendogs NintendoLand Zoo Tycoon Madden Disney Infinity Doodle Jump	Animal Crossing Pikmin Minecraft Zoo Tycoon Journey Mario Kart

Adapted from Child's Play (2017).

database which uses a point system in order to rank video games dependent upon their content and playability experiences. Using this knowledge in Child's Play, they have been able to come up with a therapeutic video game guide. The guide is freely available online at childsplaycharity.org and is updated regularly. The guide ultimately spawned from a need to provide recommendations of which video game to play dependent upon the symptoms of the child and is used as a quick reference. Ultimately they recommended that games be placed into six symptom categories of Pain, Short Term Boredom, Long Term Boredom, Anxiety/Hyperactivity, Sadness, and Cognitive Impairment. Some specific games are listed below (there are too many to list for each category entirely), but it is important to keep in mind that this list does not mean that people should be using video games for all aspects or give credence to the notion that video games are the solution to personal difficulties or should be played due to this list. This list is for informational purposes, but also specific video games the author has used as well with success.

Archetype Checklist

With video gamers playing a multitude of varying video games and each having their unique experience and environment, it is important and helpful to think of their avatars as personal representations of themselves. They may be virtual, but they are a form of them regardless of the lack of tangibility. The archetype chapter provided information about these archetypes and the following list is a useful form to use in therapy or at home when talking to video gamers. It provides ideas about their character depending on their actions, gameplay, and abilities.

Table 11.4 Video Game Archetype Checklist

Archetype	Avatar/Player Qualities
Warrior	Plays in Melee Battles, Leads the Group in Dungeons
	Uses Shields To Defend Like a Tank or Two Weapons to Attack
	Can Be Lacking in Tact and/or Aggressive Interpersonally
	Acts as a Shield for Friends/Family in Real Life
	Possibly Wants To Protect Others from Harsh Realities
	Possibly a Bully/Being Bullied

Table 11.4 continued

Archetype	Avatar/Player Qualities
Ranger	Uses a Form of Ranged Combat—Bows or Guns Used
	Usually Depicted as a Hunter or Tracker
	Tend To Be Isolative and Prefer Solitude
	Can Be Anxious about Interacting with Others
	Seen As a Watcher in Groups Occasionally Interjecting within Conversation
	Tend To Be Guarded/Wariness Interpersonally
Spell-caster	Uses Ranged Elemental Spells in Video Game Play
	Doesn't Like To Be Close Ranged/Fights from a Distance in Video Games
	Usually Knowledgeable and Curious about Others
	Introverted, But Open To Social Aspects of Life
	Seek Out Information and Guidance
	Does Not Always Like To Be Close Interpersonally
Athlete	Craves Competitive Interactions with Others in Video Games
	Generally Plays Games Requiring Quick Reactions
	Enjoys Challenges in And Out of Virtual Space
	Enjoys Completing Tasks and Attaining Achievements
	Has a Difficulty Acknowledging Personal Limits
	High Personal Drive, Occasionally Becomes Overwhelmed
Healer	Uses Healing Spells Primarily in the Video Game
	They Deem Themselves To Be Helpful to Others
	Places Others Needs Over Theirs
	Make Grand Attempts At Keeping Others Happy and Harmonious
	They Tend To Not Know Their Personal Worth While Helping Others
	Have a Hard Time With Personal Boundaries
Rogue	Stays in Shadows within Games, Prefers Assassin/Spy Play
	Uses Knives and Poisons within Video Games
	Can Be Aggressive Interpersonally, Quick To Strike Out Of Fear/Anxiety
	Players Tend To Be Cunning and Methodical, Strong, and Silent
	Does Not Like To Be in Social Spotlights Or "Seen"
	Tend To Feel Awkward In Social Encounters

Table 11.4 continued

Engineer	Methodical/Adaptive within Their Video Games
	Creative Personalities with Lofty Goals
	Controlling/Perfection Need in and out of Video Games
	Thoroughly Enjoys Puzzles and Tactful Interactions
	May Take Logic To Extreme Without Empathy/Low Emotional Warmth
	Calculating Personality Creates Difficulties When Calculations Are Wrong
Villain	Has a Boxed Like Thinking/Mentality
	Believes Only One Way To Move Forward
	Usually Is Hurtful and Lacking in Tact
	Polarizes Themselves and Identifies an Enemy
	Usually Controlling and Manipulative In Relationships
	Has a Maladaptive Approach To Solving Their Interpersonal Difficulties

Tools for Anxiety and Depression

Many video gamers have mood difficulties or a mood disorder which hinders their interpersonal interactions. The anxiety becomes too great to handle and leads to a flight response. Depression is overwhelming and leads to avoidance. However, when the video gamer encounters a similar interaction through their choice of video games the response is different. The job of the family or therapist is to use that/those video game(s) to their advantage by taking the game mechanics and overlapping them into the real world.

As an example, some therapists have used Pokémon Go for treating social anxiety or depression by playing the video game outdoors and having to walk and also catch the Pokémon. This forces them to interact with others at gyms and Poké stops along their walk, while allowing a safe haven for them to continue on afterwards if their anxiety becomes unmanageable. A tried and true therapeutically inclined manner in which to help with social or general anxiety symptoms is exposure therapy while interacting and feeling as if one belongs is a tool for depression. In essence, exposure therapy focuses upon changing the reaction and response to an object or stimulation which is feared. Through gradual and repetitive exposure, the fear, anxiety, or phobia lessens in strength and allows the individual to learn from the experience.

By interacting with other individuals, a person begins to feel as if they belong somewhere, which in turn alleviates their isolation and difficulties with social interactions.

Using Pokémon again as an example to exemplify a different approach to anxiety/depression is to make poké balls (which are used to catch Pokémon in the video game) and then have the client catch real life or imaginary objects pretending they are Pokémon. These caught Pokémon can then be used as anxiety/depression moments which an individual make elicit an anxiety or depression reaction to switch the psyche to thinking they are representing the client's own anxiety. They then let the Pokémon go which in turn lets their anxiety/depression go as well as they are symbolically setting the Pokémon/anxiety/depression free. Similarly, the poké ball can be/become a totem for the individual to ground themselves in moments of difficulty by remembering how they caught and released the anxiety/depression back into the wild.

Teaching the Pokémon different moves within the game is also a way to help with in real life anxiety/depression. In order for the Pokémon to become stronger, they have to evolve and learn new moves increasing their statistics while dueling other Pokémon. Using these same principles metaphorically, one can imagine the client as a Pokémon trainer and their anxiety/depression as a Pokémon. They, as the trainer, have to then teach and train their Pokémon to harness their own power to relieve the anxiety/depression experiences thus teaching the trainer how to work with their own difficulties as well. Creating a storyline for their Pokémon additionally is another important and useful component of the game which can be used to tell a story about the client themselves effectively rewriting a difficult portion of their anxiety/depression experiences.

Another interesting component of Pokémon is players gravitate towards specific Pokémon as their favorites. They tend to choose six to twelve out of the hundreds available to be their main Pokémon. By exploring the choice of preferred Pokémon, one can learn more about the personality and self-concept of the individual playing the game, therefore unlocking new knowledge about the person and why they make specific choices within the video game.

While Pokémon was primarily used as an example of how to effectively use the game storyline for understanding and overcoming mood disorders, anxiety, and depression, every video game has a comparable manner in which to be similarly utilized. A therapist needs to be familiar with the virtual realm being played and the mechanics of the realm to bring about these different abilities. Once acquainted, creating these tools becomes much easier and quicker to comprehend.

There are several other examples. Link in The Legend of Zelda is an orphan and must overcome his own loss of family to become the hero of Hyrule. This game is particularly good for clients who are adopted or feel abandoned, helping them to see their own personal worth and power. In World of Warcraft, players chooses their own identity and character traits which can be explored further to understand the self-concept and personality of the player. Within games like Risk and Civilization, there are choices to be made while overcoming the rest of the world and monuments to be built, which increase abilities as well. Exploring these choices further with different gameplay styles is effective for understanding the individual. Every virtual world has the ability to manage and create potential for change. The key importance for therapists and parents is to be curious about the archetypal draw to the game and how it can be harnessed for interventions. By thinking of the game as a tool in which to understand the video game player, endless possibilities arise for use across environments.

Glossary of Video Game Terms

Throughout the evolution of video games and virtual worlds associated with video games, many different and wild terms have emerged which can, and in most cases will, confuse anyone talking with a video gamer if they are not familiar with the jargon or slang. The popularly used acronyms, abbreviations, and slang terms are used to express emotions, game conditions, player actions, and avatar physical conditions. This glossary of most commonly used terms is not exhaustive, but is comprehensive in nature. If a term is being used in the therapy room and familiarity with the term is not present, then this section should provide clarity.

A

AAA—Term used for large video game companies with large coffers in order to advertise their video game.

Achievement—A completion of a difficult feat in the video game, usually gives points.

Add—An additional mob joined in the attack.

AFK—Away From Keyboard, meaning you are not able to respond to messages or hails from in the game at the moment.

Aggro—Hostile aggravation and attention from a mob or enemy.

AI—Artificial Intelligence.

Alt—An alternative character to be played in addition to a video gamer's main.

AoE—Area of Effect. A term used to describe attacks affecting multiple enemies in a designated area.

Attribute—A statistic that describes the extent to which a fictional character possesses a special and natural in-born characteristic common to all characters. Examples are: strength, dexterity, intellect, agility etc.

B

Balance, Balancing, Balanced—Attributes and actions between video game characters require this in order to ensure that all characters have an equal chance.

Battle Rez, BRez—A resurrection spell cast while in the middle of a battle. Usually a limited number of these types of spells can be cast in one battle.

BBL—Be Back Later.

BIO—Short for Biological Break or "I have/will to go to the bathroom."

BOE—Bind on Equip. Refers to loot dropping off of mobs, dungeons, or bosses. The equipment will bind to a specific character when it is equipped for use.

BOP—Bind on Pickup. Refers to loot dropping off of mobs, dungeons, or bosses. The equipment will bind to a specific character when it is picked up.

Bot—An avatar being controlled by a robotic program, usually banned in video games due to overpowering character leveling capabilities.

Boss—A bigger and badder mob which takes longer to kill and usually has phases requiring specific mechanics in order to overcome it. Drops loot which is helpful to the avatars.

Buff—An effect placed upon a character that positively impacts their statistics and characteristics.

Build—A player's skills and attributes chosen for their character.

BRB—Be Right Back.

C

Camp, Camped, Camping—A player will ambush and stay around a dead player and continually kill them when they respawn.

Crowd Control, CC—An ability used to manage, incapacitate, or hinder enemy mobs.

D

Daily, Dailies—Repeatable quests the video gamer can complete usually once per day in an effort to raise reputation or influence with a specific faction.

Damager—A playable avatar which has high damage when concentrated upon a mob or boss.

DC—Disconnected from the game.

Debuff—The opposite of a buff, an effect placed upon a character that negatively impacts their statistics and characteristics.

Ding—Achieving a new level, common word placed in chat to celebrate leveling a character to the next level.

DLC—Downloadable Content.

DoT— Damage over Time. A spell that "ticks" over time and slowly takes away or adds health.

DPS—Damage per Second.

E

Easter Egg—A piece of hidden information in the game that players usually find and has little effect on gameplay.

Expansion—An addition to an existing video game also considered an Add-on. The expansion usually adds new game areas, weapons, objects, characters, and extended storylines.

F

Facepulling—When a group member accidently or purposely pulls a group of mobs, a boss, or a single mob to the group by getting too close. Hence the name Facepulling.

Farm—To stay in one place and kill the mob or pick up collectibles and materials in a single area.

Fog of War—A computer generated fog that covers unexplored areas of the map hiding enemy units and opponets.

FPS—First Person Shooter game.

FTP—Free to Play.

FTW—For the Win! An emphasis added to a comment, message, post, or communication which can be genuine or sarcastic; more likely to be used sarcastically.

G

Game Theory—The study of mathematical models of conflict and cooperation of character's abilities to produce the maximum amount of damage, healing, or survivability.

Gamer Tag—A video gamer's online persona or name that they prefer to be called by while playing in game.

Gank, Ganking, Ganked—When an opponent used underhanded means to defeat or kill a less experienced, geared, or knowledgeable player.

Gear—Apparel, accessories, weapons, and other trinkets worn by the character played. It becomes more powerful as the game progresses and adds additional stats to the character making them more powerful as well.

Ginvite—A guild or group invite.

Glass Cannon—When a character or component of a video game has supreme firepower, but no defense meaning it can create much damage, but is weak and easily destroyed.

Gold—In game currency used to purchase items of value. Gold is the most commonly used currency, but it is possible to use other forms as well.

Griefer, Griefing—When a player intentionally causes another player grief through camping, harassment, or ridicule.

Grind, Grinding—Slowly increasing your reputation or influence with a faction, it takes a while.

Grouping—Video game players enter a group with one another in hopes of accomplishing a goal. These are not random and are more specific.

Guild—A group of members and friends which play the video game together. Usually has a hierarchy within itself.

H

Healer—A class that heals the rest of the group and keeps everyone alive.

Hitbox—An invisible box where the player can hit the enemy, if outside of it, the player will be unable to hit the mob.

HoT—Heal over Time. A spell used by healers which "ticks" and heals a character or avatar often and multiple times over the course of game and spell specific timeframe.

Hotkey, Hotkeys—Shortcut keys or a combination of keys providing quick access to functionality within a video game.

I

INC—A monster or group of mobs which are inbound to your location.

K

Keybinds, Keybinding—The practice of assigning various abilities upon the keyboard allowing an individual to hit one key to complete multiple commands or ease the use of abilities.

Kill Stealing—Arranging to kill an opponent a second before another player and obtaining the credit for killing the monster.

Kiting—When a player uses ranged attacks to continuously knock back an opponent.

L

Lag—Slowing of the game due to excessive memory, low internet connection, or poor working computer. Usually occurs when the in-game scenario or environment has high resolutions and is graphic intensive. A moment experienced when there is a large amount of latency.

LFG—Looking for Group.

Linear Storyline—The story follows a specific trajectory with little room for deviation.

LOS—Line of Sight. You have to be able to see who you are healing or damaging.

Loot—Clothing, apparel, accessories, and weapons which drop off of dungeon bosses, mobs, or AI characters.

Ludology, Ludologist—The study of games. A video game researcher.

Lust, Lusting—A spell used to increase specific abilities for a short period of time.

M

Main—A video gamer's most frequently played video game character.

Maxed—The end result of researching or reaching the maximum level and attributes a character, weapon, or statistic can attain.

Min-Maxing—The practice of creating and playing a character or avatar with the intention of minimizing undesired or unimportant traits while maximizing desired ones.

MMO—Massively Multiplayer Online game.

MMOFPS—Massively Multiplayer Online First Person Shooter.

MMORPG—Massively Multiplayer Online Role-Playing Game.

Mob—A dangerous monster who will attack you in the game.

MOBA—Multiplayer Online Battle Arena

Mount—Noun: a rideable avatar usually increasing ground speed and decreasing travel time. Verb: the act of riding an avatar.

N

Nerf—When abilities have been reduced and effectiveness in battle is no longer difficult or worth playing the character.

Ninja'ing—When another individual "steals" loot from a slain monster, treasure chest, or mob.

Noob, Newb—a new player, considered to be lame and not worth anyone's time.

NPC—Non-Player Character, controlled occasionally by AI.

O

OOM—Out of Mana, used to signal no more usable substance to usually heal a party or group member.

OP—Overpowered.

OMW—On my Way,used to tell a group that you are on the move to a specific location.

P

Pat—Patrolling mob.

Patch—An update to a game specifically aimed at fixing bugs, balancing characters, and content is added.

PC—Player Character.

Pleb—Shortened version of Plebian. Used to denote a lesser skilled player similar to noob or newb.

Premade—A premade group which is usually balanced due to being premade and gathers to accomplish a goal.

Profession—A specific area of expertise of virtual craft making. Allows the player to craft supplies, gear, and weapons which can then be sold to other players for a profit. Examples include blacksmithing, leatherworking, mining, herbalism, skinning, etc.

PUG—A group of players who gather together and are not always balanced collectively for a purpose found in the game.

Pulling—When a group pulls a mob, boss, or set of mobs with the intention of letting everyone know to be ready to fight.

PVE—Player versus Environment.

PVP—Player versus Player.

PWN or PWND or PWNED—Originally a typo derived from the word "own," but changed and accepted by video gamers everywhere. Usually used in reference to achieving a win over an opponent or player.

Q

Quest—A mission in the video game which rewards experience or gear.

Que, Queue, Queuing—Signing up to wait in virtual line to be placed with a random group of other individuals to accomplish a goal, dungeon, or raid.

R

Rage Quit—Quitting the game in an act of rage.

Raid—A mission requiring many video game players in order to accomplish the goal.

Reputation, Rep—Your influence with a faction. Having it high usually gives bonuses in gear or trinkets.

Rez—Resurrection.

RL—Real Life, commonly used as IRL meaning "in real life" meaning outside of the virtual space.

RNG—Random Number Generator.

RPG—Role-Playing Game.

RP—Role-Playing.

RTS—Real Time Strategy.

S

Sandbox—An open ended video game where the player can go anywhere in the game with minimal restrictions.

Scrub—A player who is not good even after learning how to play the game.

Season Pass—An additional purchase to the game which allows access to all DLC without further cost.

Skill Tree—A gaming mechanic for the avatar or character which consists of a series of skills which can be earned through leveling up in the game.

Skin, Skins—A graphic or audio file used to change the appearance of a character, mount, weapon, or companion.

Spawn—A place where a mob, enemy, collectible, or NPC appears in the game.

Splash Damage—When multiple enemies are hit simultaneously with one attack.

Stats—Personal statistics of a character. Some characters require specific stats in order to become more powerful while others do not help in any capacity.

Stun—To put another character into a dazed, semiconscious, unmovable, and temporarily state of shock halting all spells, actions, and moves for a short period of time.

Stun-Lock—The art of chaining up abilities in order to completely prevent an opponent from using any actions.

T

Talents—An attribute or characteristic an avatar can have. Usually a character has access to multiple talents at once and increase in power as the character levels up.

Tank—A heavily armored fighting lass which limited magical abilities and leads the group around the dungeon, raid, or zone absorbing the brunt of attacks.

TCG—Trading Card Game.

Technology Tree—Branching series of technologies which can be researched to make a player more powerful.

Theorycraft—Analysis of video game attributes mathematically to determine optimal performance.

Tick—The moment when a spell either heals or damages a character.

Toon—A character or avatar in the game.

Trash—Mobs found in dungeons and raids which are more of a nuisance to exterminate in order to get to the boss.

Troll—An individual who sows discord and discontent on the internet by starting arguments to upset other people. Usually achieved through griefing, posting inflammatory, extraneous, or off topic messages in an online community.

Twink—A low level character which has gear superior to the average player at that level. Usually used in PVP environments to overwhelm the opponent.

TYT—Take Your Time.

U

Ultimate—Powerful abilities only available to a hero, avatar, or character once their ultimate meter has filled or a specific amount of time has passed.

W

Wipe—A situation where the entire party or raid is killed in combat.

Woot, WOOT!—Success! We defeated the monster or obtained a goal and I am celebrating the victory.

World—A series of levels that share a similar environment or theme.

WTB—Want to Buy.

WTS—Want to Sell.

WTT—Want to Trade.

X

XP—Experience Points.

Z

Zerg, Zerging—When the player overwhelms the opponent purely with numbers of minions or attacks.

Zone—An area in the game where you quest or gain experience to progress through the video game. As the character levels, they can traverse new zones which would have been too difficult before.

INDEX

Locators in **bold** refer to tables and those in *italics* refer to figures.

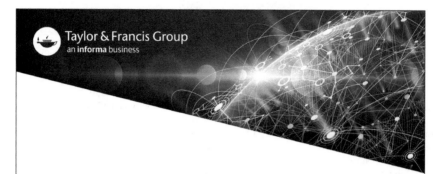

PGMO 06/26/2018